THE GOD
INSTINCT

THE GOD
INSTINCT

Heeding Your Heart's Unrest

TOM STELLA

SORIN BOOKS   Notre Dame, Indiana

www.sorinbooks.com

International Standard Book Number: 1-893732-49-5 CB
                                      1-893732-32-0 PB

Cover design by Jane Pitz

Text design by Brian C. Conley

Printed and bound in the United States of America.

Library of Congress Cataloging-in-Publication Data
Stella, Tom.
The God instinct : heeding your heart's unrest / Tom Stella.
        p. cm.
 Includes bibliographical references.
   ISBN 1-893732-32-0 (pbk.)
          1-893732-49-5 (CB)
   1. Spiritual life--Christianity. I. Title.
   BV4501.3 .S74 2001
   248.8--dc21

                                                    2001003049
                                                    CIP

By means of all created things, without exception, the divine assails us, penetrates us, and molds us. We imagine it as distant and inaccessible, whereas in fact we live steeped in its burning layers.

—Teilhard de Chardin

To my parents who, without knowing it, taught me that spirituality is a down-to-earth affair. And to the Thursday night "seekers" group, my soul mates in the quest for *meaning in the madness.*

$\mathcal{C}ontents$

$\mathcal{A}cknowledgments$

It has been said that "it takes a village to raise a child"; the same applies to the writing of this book!

I am grateful for and indebted to many people for their generous assistance, guidance, and encouragement. I begin by mentioning those who have shared their wisdom with me in the role of spiritual director: Bill Toohey, CSC, Morton Kelsey, J. Ripley Caldwell, SJ, James Finley, Fritz Pfotenhauer, and Rose Annette Liddell, SL, have all taken me farther along the spiritual path. Each in their own way has helped me see and surrender to God incarnate in the world, in others, and in myself.

Over the past twenty-five years, the Trappist monks of Our Lady of the Genesee monastery have welcomed me into their midst many times. Both they and the place they call home have made God a more tangible reality for me.

I began writing this book in Genesee, New York, continued it in Detroit, and brought it to conclusion in Colorado Springs. In each location I relied on the computer skills of others since mine are almost nil. My brother and sister-in-law, Bob and Joanne Stella, transferred hand-written notes to screen and disk. Beverly Stella, my sister, and Jeffery Glenn, my nephew, did the same with my changes to the text. Jeff Tschida, Neil Wack, CSC, and Nate Wills, CSC, typed patiently and professionally as I dictated *ad nauseam*. I entrusted what I thought was a finished product to my long-time friend, Ray DeFabio, who brought his thirty plus years experience as a teacher of English to the editing task. Jane Pitz, another friend of many years, has done for this book what she has always done with whatever her artist's hands touch—made it more appealing.

I am grateful for the support and friendship of my brother, Mike, and sister-in-law, Pat, and for James Finley again, whose word on my behalf opened the door to Sorin Books. Finally, I thank Frank Cunningham and Bob Hamma of Sorin Books for their flexibility and suggestions; this book is a better book because of them.

$\mathcal{F}oreword$

Reading *The God Instinct* brought to mind a dream a woman once told me she had while going through a troubling period in which she felt she was losing her faith in God. She dreamed of being on the farm where she was born and grew up. The details of the farmland all seemed familiar to her. But she could not find her house, which had mysteriously vanished. Searching frantically, trying to find the home of her childhood, she stumbled and fell on her hands and knees in the dirt.

This moment of falling at first upset her then surprised her with a sense of having stumbled into an unforeseeable kind of homecoming. Reflecting on this unexpected sense of homecoming helped her to see her crisis of faith in a new light. In this moment of sitting there in the dirt she sensed she was being invited to recognize and accept that the home she could not find was confining. At the same time she understood that she could learn to be at home with God in her new earthy, open to the sky situation in which anything was possible.

In these reflections I believe Tom Stella has found himself in a similar situation. The previously unquestioned way in which he had understood and experienced his faith no longer made sense to him. This experience was all the more perplexing in that he was an ordained priest, one to whom others looked for spiritual guidance.

But then he realized that this disorienting experience was, in actual fact, transformative. It opened up a new, less confining way of experiencing and understanding God's presence in his life. It is this new, earthy, expansive understanding that Tom shares with us in these pages.

As we read what he shares of his own self-transforming journey, aspects of our own journey become clearer. Each chapter sheds light on an aspect of the growing realization that life itself is a process of perpetual change that asks perpetual conversion of us. It's not a conversion from one set of beliefs to another. Rather, it is a perpetual willingness to let go of old and familiar ways of experiencing and understanding ourselves. It is a perpetual willingness to grasp the ways God is present in our ongoing self-transformation.

The God Instinct acknowledges the difficulties inherent in such conversion. It is often not easy to let go of old and familiar patterns even though they no longer conform to the changes that slowly unfold within us. While acknowledging these difficulties, this book sings with the freedom that arises when we realize that this very transformative process is woven with the mystery of God's presence in our midst.

As we read along, we are reassured of the wondrous nature of this path where deeply accepted bewilderment ripens into awe; where deeply embraced but unanswered questions ripen into humility; where the painful experience of losing old and familiar ways of understanding and experiencing God's presence ripens into an unexpected realization that we are at home with God in the intimate details of daily life.

In Tom Stella's writing you will find insights into what it means to be faithful to the unresolvable, open-ended matters of the heart where God keeps showing up in unexpected and delightful ways.

James Finley
Author and
Psychologist

Introduction

"How do you find God?" was a question once posed to Holocaust survivor and Nobel laureate Elie Wiesel. He responded, "You ask how I find God, I do not know how but I do know where—in my fellow man."

How do we find God? Who is the God we seek? Where do we look when we search for the Divine?

These questions, and others like them, have both intrigued and plagued me my entire life. They are good questions, critical questions, but the answers to them are elusive. At times these questions created in me a discontent with the reality of everyday life because I assumed that the object of them was a reality separate from life. What mattered most, I thought, was a Being in a place (heaven) beyond this place, in a time (eternity) beyond this time. This God intervened periodically and influenced the course of events, but existed apart from them.

My religious tradition reinforced these assumptions and provided answers to my questions, and I relied upon and found security in these answers for many years. But the more I experience life the less convincing I find those answers.

I have felt God's consoling and challenging presence here and now. I have seen bad things happen to good people. I have found some of life's most significant occurrences and decisions to have at least a hint of gray. And I know holy people who do not believe in God.

I have fewer answers than ever, but a better sense of the Truth. I continue my questioning but my perspective is different. My impulse now is to view questions about God, humanity, and life not as separate questions about separate realities, but as one question about aspects of the same mystery. I feel, as does Wiesel, that the place to find what I long for is here. Divinity lurks omnipresent in our midst. I believe with Thomas Merton, a Trappist monk whose life and writings continue to influence thousands some thirty years after his death, that spiritual growth is not a matter of going from question to answer, but from question to question. The search for answers is unsatisfying. The quest for Truth is unending.

I am amazed and encouraged by the number of people I encounter who, in searching their hearts and questioning the conventional dictates of church and society, arrive at this conclusion: humanity in all its messiness is holy, life with all its crazy twists and turns is a sacred affair, and the reality referred to by the word God is the holy/sacred center of all that is. Those who hold these beliefs are seekers of the truth, people who search for ultimate meaning and spiritual experience in the midst of the everyday. Their intuitions tell them that there is a hidden richness in the sometimes grind-like existence of living in the world, an existence that consists of meeting responsibilities, tending relationships, making ends meet, and dealing with all the other unpredictable and inevitable circumstances that affect our health and happiness.

I have discovered that many of the people burdened and blessed with a sense of life's sacredness are spiritually homeless and hungry. We—I count myself among them—do not seem to find the places or people who share our deepest beliefs. Even those who are church-involved come away from worship services unfulfilled because institutional religion generally reinforces the conventional view that heaven and earth, the sacred and the secular, Divinity and humanity are separate realities.

Seekers long for affirmation of our *holy hunch* that creation is the venue of the divine, that God is the essence of us. But because our spiritual perspective is not mainstream we can begin to doubt that what we sense about God and life is true. We often feel that there is something wrong with us for thinking what we think, needing what we need, and not believing what we once believed. We can be tempted to abandon what we know with our hearts is the reason for our existence—the endeavor to discover God in our midst.

Even when we are comfortable believing differently than we once did or than others do, we can lose touch with what defines that difference. This happens when we get caught in a cycle of chaotic activity. We enter into routines that become ruts. We carom from one thing to the next and arrive at the end of a day physically, emotionally, and spiritually exhausted. We lose a sense for the hush in the rush, the sane and quiet center that is the Essence of us. We become burned out.

But even in that spent state there are sparks. There are embers that may be no more than a fleeting sense that our individual lives and life itself are more than meets the eye. And so we continue to pursue the truth we intuit. And as we do we hope to stumble upon others who share our beliefs and are committed to a path of spiritual growth and discovery. I write to affirm us. I write to fan that flame of awareness, that divine "heartburn" which persists as an inner-longing, a gnawing intuition that knows with fragile but persistent certainty that God is our Essence.

I hope that what is written here will be like a gentle blowing on those faint embers that sense the preciousness of the present, the depth of the daily, the loveliness of this life, the holiness of our humanity. I hope too you will recognize your own questions, longings, and insights in these pages. I hope you will be confirmed in your quest for the infinite in the intimate and everyday dimensions of your life.

A word about content and terminology. The chapters that follow focus on aspects of life that have some significance for those who intuit God's indwelling, and about which they might have an unconventional understanding. I have attempted to address these topics in a way that reflects the perspective of those who recognize and resonate with the spiritual dimension of life.

Because Christianity is the tradition with which I am most familiar and by which I am most influenced, my source material is largely from Christian writers. But I have discovered elements of the truth I long for in many other religious/spiritual teachings and have drawn from them as well. The mystery of life's sacredness is vast, the avenues to it are many.

Because spiritual longings cut across and beyond religious lines, I have chosen a variety of terms to refer to that reality for which, I believe, we all yearn. I use the traditional designation "God" most often, but since this word usually implies an entity that is separate from life I have also engaged the terms Essence, Mystery, Divinity, Spirit, the Holy, Being, Presence, and Ground in an attempt to convey the great truth that what we have been taught is only beyond us is also within. The reality to which all these words refer is the deepest dimension of creation, the heart of our humanness. We embody what we seek, what we long for is the Essence of us.

Genesee Abbey
Piffard, New York

$\mathcal{G}od$

T. S. Eliot once stated that there are some things about which nothing can be said and before which we dare not be silent. Though these words apply to many things—life, death, and love among them—they are most pertinent to that mystery we call God.

In some of the retreats I conduct, I write the word "God" on a blackboard and ask the participants to say the first thing that comes to mind. This is especially interesting when I ask them to respond with their earliest associations; what did they learn, hear, think God was like when they were children? Words like loving, friend, and forgiving are always forthcoming, but the preponderance of their comments are usually more harsh. Judge, fearsome, distant, bookkeeper, taskmaster are common; everyone, it seems, grew up with ideas and feelings about God that were less than inviting, that created a preoccupation with sin and an obsession with salvation.

For many who are influenced by mainline religious teachings, the word God conjures up images of an old, bearded man enthroned amidst clouds and surrounded by angels. Whether punitive or loving, this God has a will (agenda) that constitutes the right way for us to live. Religious ritual, prayer, purity, and acts of charity comprise the means to please or appease God; contrition and penance are the requirements necessary to make up for our faults and failings.

A theistic understanding of God (one that imagines God to be a distant and demanding Supreme Being) is deeply embedded in our hearts as well as our minds; this is because it was not merely learned, it was "breathed in" as was the guilt that hovered, ever present, around it. Though God was thought to be at a distance, the divine vantage point enabled God to see it all: actions done, thoughts entertained, feelings and sensations experienced. The "eye" of God missed nothing. The wrath of God was easily evoked. The judgment of God was swift and unbending. There was, of course, a gentler side to God, but fear is a primary emotion, and for many it has left a lasting impression of God as an ominous figure to be either tiptoed around or approached only with an awareness of our unworthiness.

Despite their lingering presence, these stereotypic notions of God are no longer viable for many who seek to live in relation to the spiritual dimension they sense in themselves and in all creation. Mythologist Joseph Campbell has stated that theological language does not denote, it connotes. God is a word that has come to refer not to a separate and Supreme Being, but to the pervasive reality that is the Ground of Being, the benevolent Essence of us.

Though it may sound paradoxical, when one has come to embrace an understanding of God as the Ground of Being it is possible to be both an atheist and a believer simultaneously. This is the stance of many seekers who have come to think and to believe *outside the box*. We are atheists in the sense that a theistic concept of God can no longer be affirmed with integrity. Though once accepted without question, the idea that God is someone looking down on us, with love or with disdain, now holds no meaning. Neither notional ascent nor the gift of one's heart can be offered to God understood as a separate entity. But another sense for God may be held to and lived by, namely, God as pure Spirit, that which makes everything what it is essentially and pervades its being. From this perspective God is believed to be here as well as there, inside us as well as alongside us. The difference in these views of God is striking, but despite the fact that there is often a "how could I have ever believed that?" sense in those who have made this leap, the conversion from one notion to another is often a wrenching experience that shakes the security of our world. The growth of our faith usually involves a crisis of faith, since, in most cases, it is only after much time and grappling that the *dark gift*—the undoing of our established notion of God—is succeeded by a new concept, or by the realization that no concept is better than any concept.

Belief that God is the Ground of Being, our very Essence, implies that all images of God are ultimately inadequate, since it is impossible to imagine something that is no-thing, or someone that is no one. But because we tend to imagine the unimaginable it is easy to fall prey to the temptation to view God as a person who is like us, though bigger and better. It is natural to make "Him" into our own image and likeness. The limits of our mind and language inevitably frustrate our attempts to grasp God, but because "we dare not be silent" we rely on words, both symbolic and poetic, to describe what God is like. God is like a rock or fortress—immovable and strong. God is like the "hound of heaven"—pursuing us as we flee.

God is like a father or mother—embracing us in our need or chastising us for our disobedience. Metaphor and simile may express how we view or experience God, but the ultimate truth is that the reality we name God is always deeper and more intimate than any words or images can capture.

> Since God cannot be imagined, anything our imagination tells us about Him is ultimately misleading. And therefore we cannot know Him as He really is unless we pass beyond everything that can be imagined and enter into an obscurity without images and without the likeness of any created thing (Merton, *New Seeds of Contemplation*, p. 131).

God is to reality what flame is to fire, or water to the ocean. God is not someone distinct from what is, but the name we assign to what is, at the same time, so vast and so intimate as to be unthinkable. God is the reality of all that is real, the incomprehensible nothingness at the center of everything. God is the "isness" of all that is, Being in which all beings participate.

To put this another way, God is too true to be good! The word "God" refers to a dimension of reality that is beyond description, even by our best words, our most lofty notions. A positive, theistic understanding of God is that "He" is too good to be true; that is, God loves us though we have not acted lovingly, or forgives us even though we continue to sin. Such an understanding is, I believe, closer to the truth than one that imagines a conditional God whose love and forgiveness depend upon our compliance to specific norms and teachings. But even a positive image of God, if taken literally, is inadequate. God is too true to be good—too real, too one with us, too much a part of what is happening to be separate from what happens. To believe that God is not a being separate from us is to know that God neither causes nor allows the events that comprise our life; rather, God is one with them, radically present and unconditionally incarnate.

Two things must be clarified when speaking of God as being too true to be good. First, this does not mean that God is impersonal, a something instead of a someone. Seekers generally believe that the word "God" refers to a reality that is personal, though not a person. To say that God is personal but not a person means in part that we assign personal qualities, such as love, mercy, anger, or jealousy, to our sense for God. It also means that we can relate to God both within and beyond ourselves. Our relationship with God is not person to person, but person to Mystery. We are not *in* a relationship with God; we *are* a relationship, a dimension of God. God is known with the heart's mind and seen with faith's eyes to be the Essence of each breath and every step we have ever taken or will take. The omnipresent nature of Divinity is recognized as touching the deepest reaches of thoughts and feelings unknown to any other person. The very "trueness" of God enables a commingling union that is closer than close, nearer than near, above, beyond, beneath, yet utterly within the experience of human intimacy.

The second point of clarification has to do with communication. Because the word God refers to a personal reality, God can be addressed. We can have a chat with God, letting God know what is on our mind or giving God a piece of it! We can listen with the ear of our hearts to what God speaks in us. We can say that a personal God knows us with a kind of carnal knowledge, an intimacy beyond words, and by consulting the deepest level of our being we can discover God's guidance in our lives.

I have had several experiences of God's intimate knowledge of me and God's guiding presence. The first took place as I was walking across the campus of the University of Detroit. Though I wasn't thinking about it at the time, I had been pondering whether to apply for entry into the seminary. From somewhere inside me I heard the words "What are you waiting for?" I knew intuitively the meaning of those words and the source of them. Years later, I was walking the road between the church and the retreat house at Genesee Abbey, the Trappist monastery where I began writing this book. I had an overwhelming sense that God knew me, was fully present in my walking, and had a "design" for my life. This was not a divine plan, but a loving intention. Not a blueprint to which I must conform in detail, but an imprint to which I must be faithful in order to be truly free and fully alive. I sensed in this revelation that I never had been or ever would be alone. We may be deaf to what God is saying and ignorant about where we are being led, but a "too true to be good" God is never out of touch with us and is constantly guiding us along life's path. Prayerful discernment and dialogue with others are the ways to discover where the usually subtle nudgings of God are moving us.

If God is the personal Ground of Being, intricately one with all that is, then life cannot be separated into sacred and secular, holy and profane, divine and human, supernatural and natural. Because God is a name for the Essence of us, everything that is is holy. "The forms and individual characters of living and grow-ing things, of inanimate beings, of animals and flowers and all nature, constitute their holiness. Their inscape is their sanctity" (Merton, *New Seeds of Contemplation*, p. 30). Life in all its ordi-nariness, reality in all its realness, and people in all our human-ness are holy ground because the Ground, the Center, the Substance, the Essence of us is the mystery we call God. The term supernatural does not refer to a plain above and beyond nature as we know it and are it, for the supernatural is the full-ness of nature, the totality of our being. This is not a New Age concept; it is age old, a fact attested to by Irenaeus, a second-century saint of the Catholic church who said, "The glory of God is man fully alive," and by St. Athanasius who stated, "God became human that humans might become God."

Divinity is the completeness of humanity. The natural is the supernatural in the process of becoming. God is the "inscape," the interior spiritual territory, of all that is. We are the temples where, in the words of Thomas Merton, the Essence of us "sleeps in our paper flesh like dynamite."

$\mathcal{P}erson$

John Donne has written that God is so omnipresent that God is an angel in an angel, a stone in a stone, and a straw in a straw. It seems consistent with the spirit of his words to say that God is a person in a person; Divinity lies at the heart of humanity.

The word "person" is formed from the two Latin words, *per sonare*, which mean "to sound through." Everyone is someone through whom something resonates. We are like an instrument whose being is the means through which the mystery of music is manifest. Annie Dillard gives voice to this truth when she writes: "Something pummels us, something barely sheathed. Power broodes and lights. We are played on like a pipe; Our breath is not our own" (p. 13). What a mystery it is to be a person. It can be a painful mystery, as we are often out of tune, but a mystery nonetheless, for what "pummels" us and "plays" on us does so from within; it is the Essence of us. A person is an instrument through which the music of Divinity emanates. Our lives disclose God.

A person is sacred because humanity is first and foremost spiritual. "We are not human beings having a spiritual experience," says priest-paleontologist Pierre Teilhard de Chardin, "we are spiritual beings having a human experience." This truth has to do with our identity. It is basic, it is primary, but most of us do not know the first thing about ourselves. We know the second and third things, that is, the biological and psychological dimensions of our being. We are aware of the condition of our bodies and the state of our minds and hearts, but we are often ignorant of the spiritual truth that is the core of our person-hood. Seekers are in the process of awakening to the realiza-tion that a person is not someone who is subservient to a Supreme Being, but someone who is a dimension of the Ground of Being. The Mystery we call God is in us as us.

A would-be monk went before the abbot of a monastery he sought to enter. "What is the greatest suffering?" the abbot asked. "The greatest suffering is hell," he replied. "No," said the abbot. "The greatest suffering is to wear a monk's robes but not to have come to terms with the great matter." We suffer, our lives are less rich, our relationships are less satisfying or even harmful when we fail to know the "great matter" of humanity's holiness that lies beneath our persona, hidden by the robes and the roles we wear.

The more elaborate our garb and lofty our titles the easier it is to lose sight of the fact that our true identity and value have to do not with our social status, but with the Mystery we embody. I heard a story recently about a bishop who went to a nursing facility to visit his friend's mother. They spoke in a large parlor peopled with other residents and, during a lull in their conversation, the bishop turned to a woman nearby and said, "Do you know who I am?" She studied him intently for a few moments and then said, "No, but if you go to the front desk they can tell you there!" Surely we wear the roles of child, parent, spouse, friend, colleague, boss, and so on. Of course we wear the robes associated with these and other functions we perform, but first and foremost the self that wears them is more than them. When we make the mistake of identifying ourselves with our functions, we soon feel inhibited and limited by them. "I'm not your servant," a tired and frustrated mother exclaims to her demanding children. "I quit," announces a burned-out employee to his surprised manager. Perhaps without a word a too compliant adolescent packs a bag and leaves home proclaiming by this action that he is not just his parents' child. It may take years, but eventually and inevitably something inside of us rebels when we lose touch with the truth that who we are is more than what we are or what we do.

We find out who we are not by consulting others or by looking into the mirror, but by going to the "front desk," the hub of the operation, the center of our soul.

> The only true joy on earth is to . . . enter by love into union with the Life Who dwells and sings within the essence of every creature and in the core of our own souls.
>
> I break through the superficial exterior appearances that form my routine vision of the world and of my own self, and I find myself in the presence of hidden mystery (Merton, *New Seeds of Contemplation*, pp. 25, 41).

What we discover in the stillness and quiet of our deepest selves is that "our lives are a faint tracing on the surface of mystery" (Dillard, p. 9). What an awakening it is to realize that who we thought we were was merely the tip of the iceberg, and that what lies beneath the surface is not only vast but also divine. Each of us is, at the core of our soul, one with God. Our ignorance of this "great matter" is our sin; our awareness of it is the doorway to a richer life.

Because the holiness of our humanity is, like God, too true to be good—too close to call, too intimate to be described by any words—it can be helpful to use images in order to get a feel for its truth. When we picture the ocean with our mind's eye, we see a body of water both vast and deep with waves on its surface. The waves are in constant motion, alive as it were, and though they are distinct from the depths, they are still one reality with it. It is all salt water. Persons are like waves; we have a distinct shape and form, a life of our own, yet we are one with a greater reality. Waves are as much salt water as are the depths. We are essentially what our Essence is.

Our bodies are over seventy percent water, which explains the importance of hydration and why thirst is such a powerful craving. We long for and require what we are. Every person has an innate longing, an unquenchable thirst for God because God is our Essence. We are as spirit-filled as is the Mystery whose being is the source and sustenance of our being. It is we who breathe, but "our breath is not our own." It is we who live, but our life is a momentary manifestation of Life itself.

It is difficult to say "God is the Essence of a person" without it sounding like "people are God." It is not a question of whether we are or are not God, because the reality is that we both are and are not.

> "How does one seek union with God?"
> "The harder you seek, the more distance you create between Him and you."

"So what does one do about the distance?"

"Understand that it isn't there."

"Does that mean that God and I are one?"

"Not one. Not two."

"How is that possible?"

"The sun and its light, the ocean and the wave, the singer and his song—not one. Not two" (DeMello, p. 31).

We have no being apart from Being itself, no life apart from Life itself. Though we are not God, God is a name for the Essence of us, and thus we are not distinct from God. "Not one, not two"—we are not God, but we are not not God! Jesus hints at this mystical union when he addresses God on behalf of his disciples: "May they all be one . . . may they be one in us, as you are in me and I am in you . . . that they may be one as we are one" (Jn 17:21-22).

In the same way that Christians considered Jesus to be one with God, an incarnation of the Divine, so, Jesus indicates, all share in the mystery that is the communion of humanity and divinity. "Person" is a word for this; it is a mystical understanding of personhood, for it assumes our union with God, rather than our separation from God. It is little wonder that those who sense the truth of humanity's bond with God feel out of sync with others, for in traditional teaching and conventional thought humanity and divinity refer to entirely separate entities on entirely separate planes. From this dualistic conception flows a black-and-white view of life and religion. In this perspective a person is considered a fallen creature whose task is to become pleasing to God by attaining perfection.

Mysticism upsets this applecart and can be confusing and even threatening. Our neat categories are shattered; our familiar approach to ourselves, to others, to life, and to God is undermined by the mystery of it all. Because of this, mysticism is considered by many to be strange at best and dangerous at worst. Huston Smith has stated humorously that the popular interpretation sees mysticism as beginning with "mist," ending with "schism," and having "I" in the middle! A mystical understanding of our relationship with God is in fact a bit misty in that the boundary that once clearly separated humanity and divinity is now blurred. Having a mystical understanding of who we are and who God is can result in schism consisting not of a tear in the fabric of a faith community, but of a break from our former beliefs and, perhaps, an alienation from people who continue to hold them. Mysticism does have "I" in the middle, not the I of ego but the I of "I Am"—the name of the God Moses met in the burning bush (Ex 3:13), and the God we meet in the inner sanctuary, the burning bush of our true self.

When we are able to open our minds and hearts to the truth that mysticism reveals, then, like the sun breaking through a cloudy sky, the world is bathed in a new light. We can then see the unity that lies beneath diversity, which is the shared Essence that connects us despite our differences; we can then know the truth that we are "not one, not two" not only in relationship with our Essence, but also with one another.

Because we live not in isolation but in community, the realization of our divinity as persons affects our relationship with others. Every person is a manifestation of the omnipresent Spirit we call God; therefore, self-respect and compassion for others must characterize our lives. Every encounter with another is a sacred event; every interaction is a ritual wherein we touch and are touched by the Holy. Because of this, it is imperative that we reverence every person. We ought never to allow ourselves or others to do violence to us, and we ought never inflict, in word or action, violence on anyone else. Every person deserves our full attention as we deserve theirs. Everyone, ourselves included, ought to be dealt with in an honest and straightforward fashion. People who do not treat themselves or others with honor and reverence have not glimpsed the deepest truth so ably expressed by St. Thomas Aquinas, "Every creature participates in . . . the likeness of the Divine Essence." The Divinity of every person is the basis for all morality; the measure of our spiritual development is the quality of our relationship with ourselves and others.

The "great matter" of humanity's holiness has to do with the presence of God in us. We are persons in the fullest sense of the word because "something pummels us" and moves us to recognize and respect the mystery of our common Essence.

$\mathcal{R}eligion$

There is wisdom in the adage that even the best of friends should not talk about religion and politics, for these are not merely topics of interest about which they may hold divergent views, they are matters of personal, practical, and deeply felt conviction that govern the way we conduct our lives. As important as politics is to our existence on this planet, I choose to honor the adage, but religion is too central to our considerations to ignore.

Some of the most profoundly spiritual people I know, people of faith, integrity, and compassion, find little or no meaning in religion, religious practice, or church affiliation. "I am spiritual," they might state, "but not very religious." Sound familiar? Institutional religion can seem peripheral at best and hypocritical at worst in relation to living out our everyday attempts to be responsible, caring, spiritually attuned people. Of the three Cs of religion, creed (beliefs and teachings), cult (worship), and code (law and morality), only the latter—viewed as justice and universal love as opposed to "keeping the commandments"— has much meaning for many who search for God in the midst of life and relationships.

In my heart, I empathize with those who are not enlivened by participation in religious ritual or community, for I often find proponents of institutional religion to be more captive than free, more narrow than open, more dead than alive. But in my heart of hearts, I know that true religion, from the Latin *re-ligio* to (re-bind), has to do with nurturing the awareness of the Essence of us. It is a dimension of the human experience that can speak to the heart of who we are and what this brief experience we call life is all about. It is meant to be life-giving and can help us to forge our identity. Because this is true, it is imperative that we confront and grapple with the truths proclaimed by religion and religious institutions when they cease to make sense, for by doing so we can become confirmed in our own beliefs, practices, and conduct just as children establish both their autonomy from and relationship to their parents by dealing with, not just conforming to or rebelling against, their dictates.

Perhaps like many of you, my own faith development, influenced by my prayer, life experience, study, and dialogue with others, has resulted in holding vastly different views than I once did, views that in some cases are at variance with my religious tradition. Though there are times when I am frustrated and angry at the Catholic church for what seems to me to be its parochialism, paternalism, and intransigence, I have come to realize that my own beliefs have become stronger and better defined for my having to consider its tenets. The church, being what it is, has helped me to realize who I am, and that I have a place and a voice in the church both despite and because of my differences with it.

I have come to believe that the determining factor in how I understand and relate to religion is my notion of God. It has been said that if our understanding of God is false, the more religious we are, the worse it is! If God remains in our minds a distant someone somewhere else, then religion generally takes on the character of requirements, those endeavors or beliefs necessary to keep ourselves in good standing with God. This is the brand of religion that I was exposed to and influenced by in my formative years. It engendered in me, as it did in many others, not a healthy embrace of creedal truths, but a literalistic, and therefore limiting, understanding of faith, one devoid of appreciation for the richness of myth and story. It did not nurture a sense of ownership and participation in cultic practice, but a ritualistic observance that was heavy with a sense of obligation and guilt, a "do this or burn" mentality. The religion of requirements that shaped my life did not promote a morality based on the dignity of every person, but a moralism fueled by fear of punishment and hope for reward.

If, however, we use the word "God" to refer to the sacred living Ground of all that is, then the purpose of religion is to connect us to the deep inner truth, the "great matter" of our union with God, a connection which when lost has dire consequences:

> When an individual lacks the inner sense of being connected to God or being part of the Tao then a wound exists that the person experiences as gnawing, pervasive, persisting insecurity. . . . A person thus wounded seeks novelty, excitement, power, or prestige to compensate for a lack of joy or inner peace. Chronic anger and depression seem to hide just below the surface of the persona. . . . This wound affects the capacity to both give and receive love. Emotionally, scarcity, rather than abundance prevails, and thus joy and growth are stifled (Bolen, p. 100).

Seekers know that the "wound" we bear is our "original sin," that it comes with the territory of our humanness, and overcoming its effects is a lifelong process. The need to be reconnected to God within is a constant necessity because the reality of sin understood as ignorance of our Essence is our constant nemesis. The religious instinct to long for healing is basic, since it is only when we are one with the Divine depth of ourselves that we can be at peace and capable of functioning as fully human and truly religious persons. The persistent nature of our sin can never destroy the permanent presence of our desire for God.

Since the focus of healthy religion, one that has not lost its spiritual moorings, is God understood as incarnate in creation, then religious practice has meaning only if it addresses the reality of our true self, our relationships, our everyday lives as we live them. Religion cannot and need not be a sabbath only affair whose intent is to help us get through life unscathed by sin. It must be about passion more than piety, celebration not just obligation, life as well as liturgy. It must be a positive force, both alive and enlivening, that speaks to and about the mystery of our being, and the being of Mystery.

In fact, this is what traditional religion in its various forms has always been about. Religion becomes lifeless when it is separated from the rest of life. What we are dealing with here is what psychiatrist Gerald May calls the difference between tradition and traditionalism. Tradition, as he sees it, is the living faith of the dead; traditionalism is the dead faith of the living! Tradition feeds our souls with the faith, the stories, the hymns of our religious ancestors. Traditionalism, characterized by literalism, ritualism, and moralism, drains them with the weapons of fear, judgment, and condemnation. Religion seen from the perspective of traditionalism is an end rather than a means, and conformity to its dictates becomes the standard for holiness. Traditional religion is grounded in reality; it is anchored in the everyday. It is a means, a vehicle whose task is to deliver us to Mystery manifested in ourselves and our lives. Holiness here involves an openness to the divine depths, the sacred center of all creation.

Both religion and church are in the service of the great truth that is the Essence of us; they are complementary to the Spirit that dwells within us. An image that expresses the view of many seekers is that religion is like the banks of the river of spirituality. Banks are useless if the river is dried up, if there is no living faith, no sense of relationship with a personal God. Conversely, a river without banks, purely individualistic spirituality, lacks direction and may become a flood. Rather than having energy, the river easily becomes lifeless and even, perhaps, destructive to all in its path. Some people view the banks as confining and unnecessary, but many more cling to them, refusing the summons to dive in and live the adventure that is the spiritual life. This is not the way of those who understand God as the Ground of Being, nor is it what those whose lives inspired religious movements had in mind.

All of the great founders of religious movements have been both passionate and compassionate people. They loved what they believed and they lived what they loved. The spirit of their teachings, which have to do with the transcendent and the eminent, the spirit and the soul, heaven and earth, addresses the height and depth of what it means to be human. When too much emphasis is placed on either dimension, the dynamism that comes with their delicate balance is lost. If they could speak now, I fear some of those founders might say, "I'm glad I was Christ and not a Christian (Mohammed and not a Muslim, the Buddha and not a Buddhist)." The power that energized them and gave force to their message has too often been domesticated by their followers. No wonder those who seek to grow spiritually look beyond institutional religion for signs of life.

Religion that is not diluted by ecclesiastical or societal convention is a significant dimension of the human experience because it serves to remind us of and give expression to what is most basic to life. This awareness and its celebration remembers us to one another as people who share the same Essence, even though our beliefs about it and the names we use for it may vary. A fault of many who consider themselves spiritual but not religious is that they seek God alone; they have a private spirituality. The term "private spirituality" is an oxymoron; we are not just individuals whose being incarnates Mystery, but a people whose being is enlivened by the same Spirit. We cannot be one with a limitless God and be distinct from one another. Religion serves to rebind us not only to our true selves, but to the human community as well—a bond never really broken, but one that we, in our differences, lose sight of.

The rebinding that is religion's business takes place not in a vacuum and not only in the privacy of our souls, but in the context of places and the interaction of people. Churches as buildings, and churches as faith communities are where, through worship, social activities, educational programs, and service projects, we can participate in the communal nature of the spiritual journey. Like all human groupings, churches are imperfect entities full of petty politics and dysfunctional people. Many seekers have a love/hate relationship with the church and feel that they have grown beyond it. But, for all its flaws, it remains a powerful and positive dimension of the spiritual journey primarily because it provides opportunities for us to participate with others in the common human endeavor of seeking God.

Although many are alienated from it, institutional religion can be a viable means to individual and communal spiritual growth. In order to attract and engage those who are spiritually hungry, religious organizations must recapture the spirit of their founders and communicate their message in ways that speak to the heart of life in the here and now.

$\mathcal{S}pirituality$

More often than not, the term spirituality, like supernatural, is used to refer to a realm of existence that is distinct from this world. The spiritual life, it is thought, is another kind of life than the one we experience with its cares and concerns, its responsibilities and relationships, its demands and delights. Spirituality and unreality are generally considered to be synonymous.

A story that illustrates the fallacy of this belief concerns three monks who were praying in their abbey church. One monk felt himself rising out of his body. As he moved closer to heaven, he could see his fellow monks seated in the pews beneath him. One of the other monks was taken in reverie as he began to hear his praises sung by choirs of angels. The remaining monk was filled with distractions and could only think about how long it had been since he had eaten a Big Mac. Later that night the devil's assistant was reporting on the day's activity: "I was working on three monks who were praying in their church," he said, "but I was successful in tempting only two of them!"

Nothing could be further from the truth than to think that we must move away from our world and our body in order to be spiritual. Spirituality is less about theology than it is about ontology (being). Its primary focus is not with worship of a God who is in heaven, but with our relationship to the Essence of us, God incarnate. Spirituality refers to the sacredness that lies at the heart of creation.

In many cultures throughout history the realm of the Spirit has not been considered a reality apart from the material world but as another aspect of it, the source and foundation of all that our senses perceive; this view has been termed the "primordial tradition":

> The "primordial tradition" . . . is a way of imaging reality. . . . in addition to the visible material world . . . there is another dimension or level, or layer of reality. . . . The world of the Spirit is seen as "more" real than "this world." Indeed the "other reality" is the source or ground of "this world" (Borg, *Jesus in Contemporary Scholarship*, pp. 55-56).

Given this perspective, the thought or the reality of taking delight in a Big Mac is not divorced from the spiritual, because our appetites, all of them, are a dimension of the human experience which has the Spirit as its foundation. This truth is the point of the joke that asks, "What did the Zen Master say to the hot dog vendor? I'll take one with everything"! I'll take all that I can get. I'll taste everything the world has to offer. Give me an extra helping of joy, of sorrow, of pleasure, and of pain, because life in all its sweet and sour moments, in the very essence of its reality, is a holy hot dog, a miraculous Big Mac!

Though we often use, or misuse, people, events, and things, seeking from them the satisfaction of a spiritual hunger that is unquenchable, those who believe in life's sacredness know that savoring its delights can open the door to Mystery. If God is truly the Essence of all that is, then it is through what exists that we come in contact with God. We need look no further than the experience of love for another to see this truth at work. Lovers, at least in the initial stages of their attraction, long to lose themselves in the beloved. There is a blurring of boundaries that feels exhilarating and expansive. This loss of self in the other is akin to the "unitive experience" that is sometimes realized in contemplative prayer. Although this phase of a relationship is not love in the deepest sense, it is nonetheless both powerful and holy. It is a taste of Divinity, but just a taste, since every encounter of physical and emotional intimacy offers only temporary satisfaction and, with its insufficiency, the invitation to realize that God, the ultimate object/subject of our desires, is beyond as well as within our experience of life and love as we know it.

It is a strong temptation to think and to feel that growth in the realm of the spirit is measured by the ability to be unaffected by the boredom of the ordinary or the exhilaration of the extra-ordinary. A spiritual person, it is thought, stands aloof from the highs and lows of life, remaining serene and composed no matter what occurs. In fact, those furthest along the spiritual path are subject to intense emotions. They are free to feel and to express their feelings because they know that mature spirituality is never in conflict with being mature persons, that is, being at home with who they are. Spirituality is akin to vitality, and being fully alive requires us to be in touch with our emotions. What does distinguish spiritually mature people from those who are not is that they know that they are not what they feel; their identity is rooted in their Essence. Feelings of loneliness, anger, disillusionment, joy, contentment, and the like are accepted as part of what it is to be human and, therefore, a dimension of what it means to be spiritual.

The most significant spiritual teachers in my life do not distance themselves from their feelings, but respond to their triumphs and tragedies with appropriate emotion. They feel their feelings with an intuitive awareness that to do so is a dimension of their divinity. Jesus knew the importance of affective responsiveness and likened the spiritual immaturity of his contemporaries to those who refused to express joy or sorrow: "What description can I find for this generation? It is like children shouting to each other as they sit in the marketplace. We played the pipes for you, and you wouldn't dance. We sang dirges, and you wouldn't be mourners" (Mt 11:16-17). We are at our spiritual best when we laugh and cry, mourn and dance, for the Spirit is given expression in the height and depth of human emotion.

There are many schools of thought, many ways of understanding and applying the term spirituality, but the only way that makes sense to seekers who know God to be the deepest dimension of life is one that recognizes the union of spirituality and reality in all its earthiness. Spirituality and sensuality are sides of the same coin (life). Sensuality ought not to be considered crass, or a danger to our soul, as is the case in Puritan ethics. We are sensual beings. We must honor the needs and the limits of our bodily existence. Though disciplines like fasting and sexual abstinence can sharpen our sense of life's holiness, so can the experience of life's sweetness give rise to our awareness of the Mystery that informs it. There is an obvious importance to having control of our needs and desires, lest we become enslaved to their very real power. But an understanding of spirituality that does not encompass life as we live it, and us as we are, has at best no meaning in our daily lives, and at worst can cause us to live in the guilt and frustration of never measuring up to unreal ideals. This is not spirituality but spiritualism; it does not promote life but drains it from us.

When spirituality is divorced from the everyday dimension of our lives we are like a plant uprooted from the soil. When cut off from the source of life we tend to become lifeless, joyless, and critical. Journalist H. L. Mencken took aim at this phenomenon when he said, "Puritanism is the haunting fear that someone somewhere may be happy!" We are invited to rejoice in our own and others' happiness, not to shrink from our own or other's pain, and to recognize that living a full life and a holy life are not at odds.

As a proponent of "sensual spirituality," Merton always had a cynical response to pietistic spirituality when he encountered it among his fellow monks:

> The reader in the refectory each day announces the title of his book—"A Right to be Merry" it is called. He drops his voice ever so slightly on the word "Merry" as though to say "No! God forbid! Not a right to be merry!"
>
> If he ever reads anything about eating or drinking he drops his voice ever so slightly with the same pious fear (Eating! O Mercy! A sad necessity of our fallen nature!). But when he reads the words "die, death, dead," he lays them down squarely in the middle of the refectory with satisfaction and with finality (Merton, *A Search for Solitude*, p. 111).

We need not shy away from life in order to be holy. We do not give testimony to the Spirit when our spirits are glum. The enjoyment of what this world offers, and the recognition of its goodness is an affirmation that God is its Essence. The denial of life's goodness is a denial of its *Godness*.

Certainly there are times when it is right to be solemn, to "drop our voice" as an indication that the words we utter refer to an incomprehensible holiness. There are times as well when it is right to bow our heads and slow our pace in the awareness that we live in the embrace in the ever-present Presence. But surely it is right and good and wholly appropriate to shout, to lift our heads, and to dance as a testimony to the incarnate nature of Divinity. What German philosopher Friedrich Nietzsche said in reference to Christians could be said of the devotees of every religion: "His followers should look more redeemed!"

It has been said that a religious person believes in hell and a spiritual person has been there! I know of no other way to grow spiritually—to become increasingly aware of and in sync with the Essence of us—than by entering wholeheartedly into the sorrow as well as the joy, the pain as well as the pleasure that is life in our bodies and in the world. People committed to spiritual development do not look for difficulties or relish suffering, but they have learned that times of darkness, like dormancy in the life of a plant, are necessary for growth. We can misuse the elements of a spiritual practice (prayer, meditation, fasting, acts of charity) by attempting through them to change our life circumstances or wall ourselves off from being hurt by them. This sort of spiritualism repels those who seek to live with authenticity, for it is in the midst of life as it is, for better and for worse, that a grounded God is to be found.

> When we seek from Zen (or from any spiritual path) the fulfillment of our fantasies, we separate from the earth and sky, from our loved ones, from our aching backs and hearts. . . . Distracted and obsessed, striving for something special, we seek another place and time, not here, not now, not this. Anything but this ordinary life, this . . . nothing special (Beck, p. ix).

One indication of spiritual growth is that we sense the special nature of "nothing special" and attempt to be open to the divine depths of every dimension of life. Religious experiences or spiritual "highs," though they may be preferred, are not valued more than moments that are not charged with a felt sense of the sacred; rather, they are seen and accepted as a taste of what lies hidden beneath the ordinary.

During one of my visits to Genesee Abbey I asked one of the monks who had been there for thirty years whether he experienced a sense of God's closeness more now than when he first entered the monastery. Expecting an affirmative response, I was both surprised and consoled when he said, "No, but now it doesn't matter." It is indeed a sign of maturity to be able to go about one's business unconcerned about spiritual consolation or desolation, believing in the midst of both that God's presence is constant.

The term spirituality refers to the deepest dimension of life and ourselves—it is the bottomless bottom line of our being. Growth in this realm is a sober, sensual process that delights in this world, in our flesh, in our feelings, and in the mystery that is the Essence of us.

$\mathscr{F}a\,i\,t\,h$

"Keep the faith" was a familiar anthem of the 1960s often exchanged when those sympathetic to the forces of social change parted company. Keeping the faith meant not giving up the struggle for peace and against war, for civil rights and against prejudice, for justice and against oppression. In this context, being faithful was synonymous with working for change.

When speaking of faith in a religious sense many people use the word to indicate a body of doctrine, what they believe, and how they ritualize or practice their beliefs. Here faithfulness is synonymous with loyalty and can easily become the refusal to be open to new ways of understanding ageless truths. A faithful person in this sense is one who clings to what William James calls "second hand religion," a set of beliefs that remains unexamined and unchallenged, preserved intact from womb to tomb.

True faith is the antithesis of resistance to change, because it involves the embrace not of beliefs, but of the living God about whom the doctrines are formulated and the beliefs held. A seeker's faith is a relationship, a radical trust and openness to our Essence, and faithfulness is the lively pursuit of this sacred, incarnate reality.

Though many who search for God in everyday life are rooted in a specific religious tradition, they tend not to be defined by or confined to the creedal statements and teachings of their own or any other religious sect. Stereotypically, belief systems are felt to be limited. Rightly or not, they are thought to confine God to certain places (heaven, church) and to some people (the virtuous). This way of thinking assumes that God is on "our side" and that those who do not believe what we believe are in the wrong. It is a sign of spiritual health to rebel against parochialism and righteousness, since God is the Ground of all reality and is therefore present everywhere and in everyone. Faith in God precludes "sides," for there are many paths to the one Truth.

Faith is not something we have or can keep, for it is not some thing. This is a truth the Buddha attempted to communicate when he said, "When I say I have attained enlightenment, please do not think there is anything I have attained." A seeker's faith is not attained, contained, or maintained. It is not a body of beliefs held to unswervingly. It is, rather, a response to and embrace of what is unbelievable; it is a willingness to live in relation to the Mystery that is beyond our comprehension but which comprehends us. As we move forward along a spiritual path becoming more and more taken with the Presence that stirs within all life, we become transformed, focused, smitten, and committed to continued transformation. Our lives become faith-filled, and we become faithful to the living, dynamic Presence that summons us to live dynamically.

Faith in this sense is like being taken with an idea. First it catches our fancy; it intrigues us. Then we find ourselves mulling it over, looking at it from different angles. It consumes more and more of our thinking as we ponder ways to make it a reality. Those close to us might get upset as we become pre-occupied with it because we share less of our time and ourselves with them. In such a case it would be true to say that the idea we once had now has us. Faith that is a relationship with the living God is like this. It is so compelling, so attractive, so connected to the core of who we are that we cannot help but surrender to its power; we become more alive and more truly ourselves as we do. In the case of true faith, though, we do not lose contact with people, for faith reveals that God is not apart from but is the Essence of all. It not only compels us to live in the awareness of God's indwelling but it also propels us toward the God-filled person of others.

When we find ourselves becoming committed—be it to God, to a person, or to an idea—we sometimes express the commitment by taking vows. These promises are meant to enhance our faith but they can become, in subtle ways, an obstacle to it. The latter happens when we become consumed with being faithful to the vows rather than to that which moves us to pronounce them. During one of several meetings between Thomas Merton and the Dalai Lama, they spoke about the similarities and differences between the monastic life in their various cultures and religious traditions. Merton records the following:

> He started asking about the vows. . . . Then he said: Well, to be precise, what do your vows oblige you to do? Do they simply constitute an agreement to stick around for life in the monastery? Or do they imply a commitment to a life of progress up certain mystical stages? (Merton, *The Asian Journal*, p. 337).

In the life of one who seeks to be in tune with the Spirit, there is no contentment in merely "sticking around for life." Whether in matters of religion or relationship, it is not enough to be faithful to one's vows. The conviction and the call to live in the Mystery that lives in us is a force that compels us toward authenticity, not complacency, toward faithfulness to the spirit of our vows, not merely keeping the letter of them. I am not suggesting that keeping vows is unimportant, but that doing so is in the service of a greater good, namely, a growing sense of communion with our Essence.

Theologian Andre Louf has stated that a monk is someone who every day asks, "What is a monk?" A seeker asks not only "Who is one who seeks God?" but "What does it mean for me to be a person who does so?" What does it mean for me to be a seeker who is married, divorced, single, or celibate? What does it mean for me, a Christian, a Jew, a Hindu, or a Muslim, to be hopelessly smitten by the Divine? This is, in part, what it means to live a life of faith and faithfulness. We never stop wondering and asking what it means to be who we are, to do what we do, to believe what we believe, to vow what we may have vowed, to always be willing to be challenged and changed by the people, places, things, and experiences that happen to us along life's way. Faith does not limit our lives; it expands them. Faith invites us to seek the truth and the meaning of our existence in the ultimate truth that is our Essence. Faith affirms that who we are is intimately related to who God is.

But a life of faith not only asks, it answers. It is not only an openness to the Essence of us, but a response to it. This implies that, before anything else, a person of faith is a person who listens. We listen to the voices of people we trust, the teachings of those we admire, and the collective wisdom embodied in the doctrine of revered traditions. But primarily we listen within. "Be still and know that I am God" (Ps 46:10). When we are still, and quiet, and trusting, we discover that what we seek to be faithful to "speaks" in us:

> I don't know Who—or what—put the question, I don't know when it was put. I don't even remember answering. But at some moment, I did answer Yes to Someone—or Something—and from that hour I was certain that existence is meaningful and that my life, in self-surrender, had a goal (Hammarskjold, p. 205).

A seeker does not listen primarily for a voice from the heavens, but for a nonverbal nudging, a persistent and benevolent call from within. The "yes" that is spoken in response to it is not a word of affirmation, but a life lived affirmatively. In biblical terms it is loving God "with all your heart, with all your soul, with all your strength, and with all your mind, and your neighbor as yourself" (Lk 10:27). In practical terms it means a willingness to live with childlike vulnerability to the sacredness of every day, no matter how ordinary, to every event, whether welcome or not, and to every person, friend or foe. We answer "yes" to God when we hold nothing back from a neighbor in need, when we apply ourselves wholeheartedly to our work, even though our boss isn't looking, when we resolve to overcome an addiction by committing to a twelve-step program, or when, in the quiet of the night, we linger in an intimate stillness making ourselves available to the advances of a jealous God who would tolerate no rivals for our affection.

One might say that the "yes" of faith is what is meant by "obedience to God's will." Traditionally, this involves discerning God's plan for us and complying with it. But true obedience is not about doing God's will—it is about "being God's will." In other words, obedience to God involves being true to the reality of God's indwelling. Concretely, this means that faithfulness issues forth in a life that exhibits compassion, forgiveness, inclusivity, justice, and so on, not because God wants us to live this way, but because we are the infleshment of God who is this way. It has been said that we are as prone to love as the sun is to shine. The commandment that calls us to love is not an external law but an internal imperative, and faithfulness to that imperative is obedience to a self made in God's image. Faith in God and obedience to our Essence are synonymous. This stance is given credibility by Meister Eckhart who said, "The Ground of God and the Ground of the soul are one and the same."

A person of faith never stops asking, never stops listening, and never stops saying "yes" to the Essence of us. This is a life of faithfulness, commitment to growth and "progress up certain mystical stages."

$\mathcal{P}rayer$

" Those who speak do not know. Those who know do not speak." This timeless Taoist saying expresses the change in the understanding and practice of prayer that has taken place for many who desire an intimate relationship with the Essence of us.

Prior to any experience, relationship, or insight that may have moved us to realize that our bond with God is more personal and pervasive than we had imagined, our prayer is likely to have consisted of many words. Whether spoken or thought, we probably formulated, with words, prayers of petition, praise, or gratitude directed to a distant God and expressing deep feelings about what mattered most to us. Much of our prayer may have been the words of others, formula prayers such as the Lord's Prayer recited by Christians, the Shema of Judaism, or the Hindu Gayatri mantra.

Prayer of this sort is good, and can serve to create a sense of connection with God, a feeling that one is in relationship with what is ultimate. But for some, there comes a time when word-filled prayer whose aim is to communicate with God is no longer expressive of their understanding of themselves, life, or God. Those for whom this is true have a sense of communion with God and a oneness with life that renders words inadequate. Those who "know" this bond, who experience, however vaguely, an intimacy with the Essence that permeates all reality, tend not to speak to or think about God when they pray. For them, praying is primarily a matter of living in the embrace of God; it is being in Being. Silence, not words, breathing, not saying prayers, are more expressive of their "intuitive take" on life's holiness which is recognized to be God's venue, the holy ground of the Ground of holiness. Merton puts this playfully when he writes, "What I wear is pants. What I do is live. How I pray is breathe" (*Day of a Stranger*, p. 41). This type of prayer stresses awareness of all that comprises the present moment—sights, sounds, feelings, thoughts, actions—because the Mystery we commune with in prayer is mysteriously present in all things within and outside of ourselves. God awaits us at every turn, penetrates us with each inhalation, embraces us in every breeze.

This understanding of prayer makes it more than a time set aside to focus on God, a separate and sacred activity distinct from the rest of our lives. A seeker knows that because God is an ever-present Spirit, praying is an ever-present possibility. Because life is holy, living it is a form of prayer. Because humanity is sacred, being human is a wordless statement of communion with Divinity. Though words may be used to express our sense for this mystery, the reality of it is the real prayer. There is the prayer of our being and of our doing the things we do. There is the prayer of the sun rising and setting, and the surrendering of each season of the year to the next. There is the prayer of birth and death, health and illness, embrace and separation. And there is, hopefully, our sensitivity to the God-filled sacredness of all that is and occurs that enables us to experience life and to live in a prayerful fashion.

Though time may be set aside to rest more consciously in our relationship with God, true prayer, which is a matter of relating to God's everpresent presence, has no time limits. St. Paul speaks about this when he encourages early Christians to "pray constantly" (1 Thes 5:16). Constant prayer is not about a ceaseless flow of words, unending thinking, or abiding feelings associated with God. Rather, it is about living daily in the awareness of the godliness of life. What St. Francis of Assisi said about preaching also applies to prayer: "It is useless to walk anywhere to preach unless our walking is our preaching." If it is not evident from the way we walk, talk, work, and play that we are in prayerful relationship with the divine dimension of life, our prayer is fruitless. True prayer both informs and transforms every aspect of our lives, physical, mental, and emotional.

The transition from saying prayers to having prayer become a quiet openness to God, both during and beyond designated times, is usually a gradual movement. It is akin to the journey of the Israelites described in the book of Exodus, a journey from Egypt to the Promised Land, wandering through the desert, from captivity to freedom. Those who have made or are making this journey, who have left the comfortable though confining land that was life prior to awakening to God's omnipresence, might describe their prayer experience this way: "I used to feel close to God when I prayed but now I do not." "Prayer was always life-giving, but now it is always dry and lifeless." "Praying as I once did no longer has meaning for me, but I don't know how to connect with God anymore." Their desert of distance and uncertainty with regard to prayer and God is an invitation to growth; it is the "dark night" that summons them to realize that prayer is God's business, and that it requires surrender, not forced effort. Periods of dryness in prayer are holy times best spent with a reverent openness to what is unfolding within—especially when it seems like nothing at all is unfolding—rather than searching for new ways to pray that can help us regain a feeling of closeness to God. Feeling close to God is not the point of the spiritual life and thus not the point of prayer. Whether felt or not, intimacy with the Divine is a reality—we cannot not be one with our Essence. The journey to God is a journey with God, even when it feels otherwise.

When we have sensed the all-encompassing oneness that is life, ourselves, and God, we are moved not only to live prayerfully, but also to rest in the inner depth that is the Essence of us. In the same way that we are drawn to spend time alone with someone we love, we are compelled to withdraw from the company of others in order to savor the experience of spiritual intimacy. We may create the equivalent of a romantic atmosphere for our rendezvous with God. Finding a private place, lighting a candle or incense, allowing no rival to intrude by way of thoughts about the past or future. Only being with the beloved matters; there is no time but the present. Since "those who know do not speak," the specific time designated for prayer is a quiet time. No words need be spoken or read, no thoughts or insights entertained, no feelings, regardless how consoling, are given significance. All that really matters is that ". . . indeed He is not far from any of us, since it is in Him that we live, and move, and exist" (Acts 17:28).

If we can be said to be doing anything in this form of quiet, contemplative prayer, it is listening:

> Imagine a woman walking alone in the woods searching for her lost child. Suddenly in the distance, she hears what sounds like a faint cry for help. Just as suddenly, she stops, for now the noise of the dry leaves beneath her feet is an intolerable interference. So strong is her love that for a brief moment she stops breathing. She is a listening presence (Finley, *The Awakening Call*, p. 23).

The "noise of the dry leaves" is a metaphor. There is the noise of our worries and regrets, the noise of our hopes and dreams, the noise of our physical and emotional aches and pains, all of which can conspire to distract us from the task of listening to the faint cry of God within. But each time we become aware of the noise, we are invited to become aware again of the cry.

To listen with one's whole being is no easy task, but once aware that this is what our part in prayer requires, we can return to it when distractions beset us. Praying necessitates a constant return to the quiet consciousness of our communion with God during specific times of prayer and during the prayer that is the unfolding of life. The gentle art of reaffirming that the union with God that informs our lives persists, despite our wandering minds and hearts, must become a seeker's way of life.

> But I keep finding myself in prayer. And that is something I shall always be able to do, even in the smallest space, pray.
> Truly, my life is one long harkening unto my self, and unto others, and unto God. And if I say that I harken, it is really God who harkens inside me. The most essential and

the deepest in me harkening unto the most essential and deepest in the other. God to God.

But I refresh myself from day to day at the original source, life itself and I rest from time to time in prayer (Hillesum, p. 228).

Those who seek God keep finding themselves in prayer. Sometimes our prayer is intentional but often, without conscious effort, we become aware that we are aware of God. This awareness is often fleeting, but sometimes, in a more sustained fashion, the sense of Divinity's presence emerges, and with it an awareness of the bond that unites all creation. This gift of a felt sense of the Holy and of our communion with it can assail us at any time and place as it did the author just quoted, Etty Hillesum, a Dutch Jew who died at Auschwitz. In the midst of the most dire circumstances, she kept finding herself in prayer, growing in an awareness of the divinity of life that she listened for and heard in the painful cries of her fellow sufferers and, unbelievable as it may sound, in the person of each one who inflicted the suffering.

True prayer is less an act of communication and more a process of communing, which involves frequently returning to an awareness of the Essence of us, while listening for God in the midst of our activities and apart from them.

$\mathcal{W}onder$

A group of men who earned their livelihood as porters were hired one day by people who had come to their country for a safari. The porters hoisted the heavy supplies necessary for the journey onto their backs and began the long, hot trek into the jungle. Several days into the journey they stopped, unshouldered their burdens, and refused to go on. After many pleas, bribes, and threats failed to persuade them, they were asked why they would not perform their duties. "We can't go on," one of them stated, "we have to wait for our souls to catch up with us."

Whether we carry physical, mental, or emotional burdens through life, most of us know what it feels like to be without our souls. How many of us drag ourselves through the day? How often are we numbed by the routine nature of what we do? How splintered are we made to feel by the hectic pace imposed on us by others and by ourselves? So much to do, so little time. The mystery that is life gets lost in living our day-to-day lives. The energy at the heart of our being becomes depleted by the necessity of bearing our burdens. The days become weeks, the weeks months, the months years, and we find ourselves at mid-life and beyond, wondering whether we have wasted our lives, wondering whether we should have spent more time wondering.

A sense of wonder is characteristic of those who seek God, because the desire to live attuned to life's holiness is an invitation to marvel at the Mystery that lies at the core of creation. The sense of the sacred that fuels our lives is not a reality apart from the world, but is the Essence of it. All things testify to the deeper Truth that is their inscape.

Just as when lovers look into the eyes of their beloved and often experience a sense of communion, so seekers looking upon what is can sense the relationship that unites them with what attracts them. The German mystic Meister Eckhart has said that "the eye with which I see God is the same eye with which God sees me." We are not apart from that which inspires wonder in us: "The province of the mysterious is where the distinction between subject and object breaks down. . . . 'Mysteries are not truths that lie beyond us: they are truths that comprehend us'" (Keen, pp. 24-25). Parents gaze into the eyes of their newborn child. A tourist stands speechless at the edge of the Grand Canyon. The audience is mesmerized by the haunting beauty of a Mozart sonata. In each scenario, something within those involved is touched by something without. They are moved in a moment of recognition and relationship. Deep calls unto Deep, Spirit summons Spirit, and these observers are held in wonderment, much as William Wordsworth was when he wrote:

> . . . For I have learned to look upon nature not as in the hour of thoughtless youth. . . . And I have felt a presence that disturbs me with the joy of elevated Thought; a sense sublime of something far more deeply interfused, whose dwelling is the light of setting suns, and the round ocean

and the living air, and the blue sky, and in the mind of man; a motion and a spirit that impels all thinking things, all objects of all thought, and rolls through all things ("Lines Composed a Few Miles Above Tintern Abbey," p. 106).

Wordsworth had learned to see beneath the surface to the heart of reality; this is the secret of wonder. It is one thing to be taken by the beauty or grandeur of an object or a landscape, and another to experience a oneness with what infuses it: the incomprehensible something that is no thing, the soul of reality, the Essence of us. It is more than meets the eye. It cannot be seen, heard, or held, though everything that can be sensed or grasped is an epiphany of its unknowableness. When we fail to wonder at this dimension of existence, we fail to live fully and, according to Gerald May, we fail to achieve our purpose: ". . . the chief purpose of humankind is that there can be someone to say 'Wow!'" (p. 190).

It has probably been a while since most of us have uttered a spontaneous "Wow!" It is a word that seems more appropriate on the lips of a child than an adult. But perhaps that is our destiny, to be a child again. Jesus says, "Let the little children come to me . . . for it is to such as these that the Kingdom of God belongs" (Mk 10:14). Unless we learn to see with a child's eyes, we will miss out on the joy of wonderment. Pablo Picasso has said, "It takes a long, long time for one to become young!" Cultivating the ability to wonder is the work of a lifetime, but its rewards are reaped daily as the simplest encounters with the most familiar objects and people take on a freshness they had lost. A child's eyes give us the penetrating vision that is expressed in the saying, "If you look at a tree and see a tree, you have really not seen the tree. When you look at the tree and see a miracle—then, at last, you have seen!" (DeMello, p. 15). We have not really seen any object or person until we have seen their miraculousness. Nor have we grasped the full meaning of any element of life merely by formulating thoughts or articulating words, for as St. Gregory of Nyssa has said, "Concepts create idols: only wonder understands anything."

Wonder understands the Mystery that stands under and within every breath and beat of our heart not by digesting a book on anatomy, but by beholding the complexity and simplicity of being. Wonder understands the eternal sacredness embodied in the vastness of a clear, star-filled night sky not by comprehending the science of astronomy, but by being comprehended and apprehended by the wonder that is a night sky. Jesus alludes to the uncomplicated nature of wonder and of wonderers when he says: "I bless you, Father, Lord of Heaven and of earth, for hiding these things from the learned and the clever and revealing them to mere children" (Mt 11:25). The knowing that is the realm of the intellect need not be a barrier to wonderment, but speculation can remove us from the immediacy of experience which is the childlike heart and soul of wonder.

To be moved by any aspect of creation is a religious experience in the truest sense, because God is the Essence of all that is. It is no surprise that the word God comes easily to the lips of anyone who brushes up against life's mysteriousness, for God is like the word "wow" in that both are exclamations uttered in response to an experience of wonder:

God is beyond all images, physical and mental. Martin Buber's understanding of the origin of the divine name Yahweh is suggestive. Buber argues that it originated in an exclamation drawn forth by ecstatic religious experience and means roughly, "O the One!" The most sacred name of God is an exclamation uttered in a moment of religious ecstasy. God cannot be named, only exclaimed (Borg, *The God We Never Knew*, p. 48).

We encounter God in nature, relationships, and the various events, large and small, that comprise our daily life when what, to our eyes, appears to be a mountain or a river is recognized in its fullness as an epiphany, or when a person is seen not only as a flesh and blood human being, but as an incarnation of the Divine manifesting God's presence and action in the world. There is no corner of our existence that is devoid of the Holy, no niche from which God is absent. When we enter into our lives with a sensitivity to this truth, the Divine can emerge from its hiding place in the ordinary and take our breath away with its subtle sanctity.

Looking for the Holy in life is not about seeing visions or other extraordinary phenomenon, since reality as it is, is replete with the Divine. The ordinary workings of life contain wonder enough, for they reveal the truth that all life is holy. "A mature sense of wonder does not need the constant titillation of the sensational to keep it alive. It is most often called forth by a confrontation with the mysterious depth of meaning at the heart of the familiar and the quotidian" (Keen, p. 23). True wonder is subtle in nature because the Mystery that is its source permeates reality; it is buried in the being of things and easily goes unnoticed because it is their Essence and ours. The "wow" that is a response to detecting the innate holiness of the ordinary is sometimes a "whispered wow" because the catalyst for it is often undramatic. Like a warming ray of sun, a soft breeze, or a gentle voice, the unleashable power of Divinity leaves its indelible mark on our soul by barely brushing our being. An indication that one is growing spiritually is not evidenced by the frequency or intensity of religious experiences, but by the capacity for being smitten by the subtle holiness of life in its everyday simplicity.

In a letter she sent to me some years ago a friend shared the experience of awakening to the wonder of her life in the midst of very ordinary circumstances:

> It's kind of hard to explain, this sort of pervasive feeling of well being. It struck me this evening while I was putting clean sheets on my bed, and again while I was washing the bathroom mirror, and again as I finished the dinner dishes. All ordinary, all things that I do at least weekly, some daily, all things I have passionately resented doing at various times. But tonight for some reason, their ordinariness seemed almost glorious, like I was exactly where I belonged, doing exactly my part in the universal order at that moment. . . .

This kind of experience can happen to anyone, anywhere, at any time. It may happen only once in a lifetime, but what is important is not whether it remains or recurs, but whether, having known a moment like this, we then live in such a way—reverent and ready—as to taste it again should it emerge.

Periodically we say, or hear others say, in reference to a significant opportunity, this is the "chance of a lifetime." Those who have sensed the Mystery in our midst know that our being, and the reality of all that is, is the life of a chance time! Given what we now know about physics, evolution, and the existence of a universe whose vastness is without end, isn't it amazing that life is? What a stroke of luck or fate that conditions are such that reality in its many forms exists. The chanciness of life is not a denial of God's creativity but an affirmation of the ongoing nature of it. Creation was not a "once upon a time" phenomenon; it is a moment-by-moment mystery alive and evolving in both predictable and unpredictable ways. God is one with the process, not a being causing it from afar, but the Essence of it. It has been said that coincidence is God's way of remaining anonymous! The reality of creation and the wonder of each day's unfolding, for better or worse, is a God-filled, sacred randomness; it is the life of a chance time that is never without purpose and direction because it is all meant to open our eyes, to expand our minds, and to break our hearts in wonder.

The mystery of all that is invites us, by being what it is, to wonder at the fact that, as I write these words and as you read them, we exist on a planet that is spinning on its axis, revolving around the sun, and is situated in a galaxy that, for all its vastness, is a mere speck in the entirety of the universe. How did this come to be? How does this continue to function? What does it mean that we are part of it and that, too soon, we will cease to be? There are scientific, philosophical, and theological responses to these questions, but in the last analysis they are mind-boggling and wonder-filled quandaries.

Creation does not have to be, but it is. We are temporary, but we are. Our individual lives may be trying and trivial at times, but life itself is never other than the miracle of Mystery manifest, the holy Essence of us made available to our senses. "Wow!"

$\mathcal{C}_{ontemplation}$

Contemplation is a word with many meanings. In the realm of religion it is a form of meditative prayer, a wordless, thoughtless resting in the presence of God. It also refers to a process that seeks to plumb the depths of a significant experience, circumstance, or life decision. In relation to the spiritual life, contemplation is a way of seeing and of being in the world. It is about gazing upon life with the eye of the heart, recognizing and responding to the sacred Mystery that is life's Essence. Contemplatives live with a profound conviction—not usually felt but real nonetheless—that they are one with everyone and everything in God.

> There is a sense in which it can be said that we are all contemplatives, because whether we know it or not, we are *in God*. This interiority and depth is in all of us. . . . We discover the true God at the very center of our being and ourselves as nothing apart from God (Shannon, p. 77).

Everyone is a contemplative; seekers are contemplatives who sense this dimension of themselves and are moved by this awareness to encounter life's hidden depths.

Contemplation is not primarily an activity of the mind, or a state of reverie that transports us above and beyond our earthly and earthy existence. It is a quality of presence, a vulnerability to what is unseen yet real, a whole-person communion with the deepest dimension of life. There is a silence that gives birth to sound, a stillness from which all action arises, an utter nothingness that is the font and source of everything, a holiness at the heart of our humanness. Contemplative persons are those who walk with a sense of that silence, stillness, nothingness as they move from gate to gate at the airport in order to make their flight connection. They know with their heart that they are part of something vast as they take the garbage out, mow the lawn, or go about the business of changing their clothes, a flat tire, or their child's diaper. Contemplative awareness is a "sixth sense," an intuitive certainty like that of a woman who, without medical confirmation, just knows she is pregnant. Contemplative persons just know that Divinity lurks within every aspect of life. This knowledge or sense does not require consciousness or felt feeling to be experienced as true, for the oneness of all creation with its Essence that a contemplative intuits is deeper than thought or feeling. It is akin to love for another which may give rise to thinking and feeling about the beloved, but is more about reverencing the sacred reality of who they are and appreciating the sacred bond that unites them with us.

There are, however, those times—usually brief but occasionally enduring—when what is not normally available to our minds and emotions pierces our awareness and undoes us with its depth. Because all of life is sacred, any aspect of it can be the occasion for this awakening. It can come out of nowhere as it did for a friend who, in a recent letter, wrote, "Every once in a while a wave of who I truly am washes over me." A simple statement but a profoundly felt experience of the Mystery at the heart of our humanity. A contemplative moment such as this reveals the truth, usually hidden from us, of what is always the case: everyone and everything is a sacrament of the Divine.

The temptation in an experience of this sort is to try to turn the "every once in a while" into a "more often than not." There is no way to accomplish this. Contemplative moments are a gift. Receptivity and gratitude, not grasping and control are a fitting response to them. William Blake states this truth in his poem "Eternity" (p. 470):

> He who binds to himself a joy
> Does the winged life destroy
> But he who kisses a joy as it flies
> Lives in eternity's sunrise.

If we are wise, we resist the tendency to squeeze those rare experiences of God's closeness, but instead learn to embrace them. For life is not only about highs, but highs and lows; it is not only about consolation, but consolation and desolation. A person who walks a seeker's path grows in the ability to sense God's presence in both extremes and in the middle ground. To live contemplatively is to be free from the hold of the experience of the Holy, and free for its next manifestation, since what is important is not that we constantly feel or are aware of the Sacred, but that we are willing to go with the flow of its holy unpredictability, to live in a manner that is consistent with the ungraspable reality it reveals.

Herein lies the difference between contemplation and wonder. Both are about being moved by the usually hidden holiness of life, but contemplation involves a response to our awakening:

> We are all of us more mystics than we believe or choose to believe. . . . We have seen more than we let on, even to ourselves. Through some moment of beauty or pain, some subtle turning of our lives, we catch glimmers at least of what the saints are blinded by, only then, unlike the saints, we go on as though nothing has happened. To go on as though something has happened, even though we are not sure what it was or just where we are supposed to go with it, is to enter the dimension of life that religion is a word for (Buechner, p. 152).

Though our terminology differs—Buechner uses "mystics" and "religion" where we have been speaking of "contemplatives" and "spirituality"—the point is the same: we are summoned by the experience of life's sacredness to walk in faith. We are challenged to order our lives around the mystery, once glimpsed, that all life is the venue of the Holy. We are invited into a contemplative way of living that is open and responsive to the truth that, in the words of Dietrich Bonhoeffer, "reality is the epiphany of God."

What does it mean to respond to "some moment of beauty or pain" that is intuited to be a revelation of Divinity? What does it mean to refuse to go on as though nothing has happened, when in fact we know that we have been summoned by what has touched us to become someone we have yet to be? What does it mean to live contemplatively? Contemplative living is marked by three characteristics: recollection, reverence, and radicality.

Recollection is about moving through life with a quiet sensitivity to the sacredness of the present moment. Never far from the awareness of the Mystery that permeates creation, those who are recollected are anchored to the core of their being, rooted in their own and life's Essence. They are not withdrawn from the day's comings and goings, but neither are they lost in them. Like the man in the Zen story who is chased by a tiger to the edge of a cliff where he jumps off, clings to a vine with one hand and with the other plucks a strawberry from its vine and savors its taste, a recollected person savors the sacredness of life's small things, even in the face of the distasteful. Despite the stress involved in a high dollar business deal she is orchestrating, a woman pauses to feel the soothing warmth of the sun on her face as she enters the workplace. Though preoccupied with his son's misdeeds, a father faces the school counselor with an appreciation for the sacred nature of parenting in good times and in bad. Contemplative recollection is possible for everyone in every circumstance, because the anatomy of every circumstance manifests the mystery that is its Essence.

A sense of *reverence* for life flows from the recollected awareness of God's incarnate presence. "Every bush is a burning bush" wrote Elizabeth Barrett Browning. To see with the eyes of a contemplative is to recognize the holy ground that is nature, including human nature. It is a recognition of the sacred that draws us, like moths to light, into a relationship with what embodies that sacredness. Living reverently implies caring for, not just about, our environment and caring for, not just about, those who share it with us.

Perhaps the most profound act of reverence is a bow. To bow to a person or an object is to honor their sacredness. Living reverently compels us to bow often, if not physically then interiorly, as we sit before the food we are about to eat, as we answer the phone or doorbell that disturbs our quiet comfort, or when we enter into a difficult dialogue with our spouse, child, neighbor, or colleague. Contemplative reverence moves us to do these things with a gentle and full presence to what we are about, based on the belief that in everything we do and in every person we encounter, we are face to face with God.

A contemplative life is a *radical* life, one that cannot remain still or silent in the face of disorder. We are one with the universe and with every person who shares it with us. If we have a sense of recollection and reverence we will be moved to speak and act on behalf of the powerless and oppressed, for though they may be separate from us, they are not distinct from us. Though he or she may be still within, a contemplative is a hell raiser, one who challenges the status quo and who does his or her part to transform the hell of unjust structures while assisting those who are victims of them.

This dimension of contemplative living was evident in the life of Thomas Merton who, from the seclusion of his monastery, challenged a nation to take civil rights seriously, to consider the horrors of nuclear war, and to reevaluate its participation and escalation of the war in Vietnam. Mohandas Gandhi, Dorothy Day, Martin Luther King, Jr., Cesar Chavez, and Mother Teresa were also people whose contemplative sense for the holiness of life moved them to take a radical, nonviolent stance on behalf of the victims of injustice. The usually calm and gentle demeanor of contemplatives cloaks a power and tenacity born of conviction about our shared Essence. Theologian Karl Barth has said that "to clasp the hands in prayer is the beginning of an uprising against the disorder of the world." Whether in the monastery or the marketplace, contemplatives do what they can to right wrongs with prayer, with action—with both.

Contemplation involves an awareness of the hidden holiness of life. It knows and gives witness to our oneness with God and moves us to live lives of recollection, reverence, and radicalness based on the fact that we share a common Essence.

$\mathscr{P}resence$

Have you ever "come to" while driving your car? I would wager that ninety-nine percent of us have had this experience of realizing, after an undetermined amount of time and distance, that we are where we are—behind the wheel of a speeding automobile.

This is a rather dramatic example of what is more often a subtle reality—seldom are we consciously present to the present, to the common but potentially rich activities that comprise our lives. We are prone to doing one thing and thinking about another; this is especially true about those things we do often and automatically, everything from brushing our teeth to the "Hi, how's it going?" greeting directed to a neighbor or colleague to which we do not expect, nor do we usually want, any response except "Fine, how are you?" From a practical perspective this absent-minded way of living can be dangerous because accidents happen when we are not conscious of where we are and what we are doing. Spiritually it is problematic because we miss out on the richness of the moment, the Essence of us that lies beneath our everyday activities and relationships: "we are looking for that radiance in all things that mystics call the face of God. That radiance is not hidden in some far-off place, but is here and now right under our noses" (Beck, p. 262). Whether it is referred to by the Buddhist term "mindfulness" or its Western counterpart "recollection," there is nothing more basic to a seeker's life than being present to the present.

In the lore of Hasidic Judaism is a story that illustrates this truth. There was a rabbi who had a recurring dream in which he saw himself going to a distant country where he would discover a treasure buried beneath the castle of the king. He ignored the dream at first, but after being visited by it a third time, he packed his bag and journeyed to that land. All was as it appeared in his dream, except that a guard stood watch before the bridge leading to the castle. The rabbi paced back and forth all day pondering his dilemma until finally the guard asked him who he was and what he was doing there. The rabbi told him about the dream, and the guard laughed scornfully. "Old man," he said, "if I had been a believer in dreams, I would have listened to one I had years ago. In it I saw myself going to a distant country to the home of a rabbi where, beneath his house, I discovered a great treasure."

Within the within of our own lives lies the treasure of joy, peace, and meaning that we usually look elsewhere to find. It is out there, we imagine, in that other person, that other job, or in the next life, heaven. St. Catherine of Siena has said that "all the way to Heaven is Heaven." Thoreau says that "Heaven is under our feet as well as over our head." Heaven is a metaphor for the fullness of life that is our deepest yearning. One who seeks God in life senses that this fullness is not just a reality hidden in some distant place and time, but the fruit of living in the here and now, the bliss of discovering in the present the presence of the Essence of us.

The thought of discovering a buried treasure is exciting, the thought of digging for one is less appealing. In one of Aesop's fables he tells of a wealthy farmer who on his death bed informs his sons that there is a treasure hidden in the cornfield. After his death his sons dig throughout the field but find nothing. Though discouraged, they decide to plant corn since the soil was now tilled; when their efforts yielded a bumper crop they realized the meaning of their father's words. Presence to each moment and event in our lives is to the discovery of God what digging was to the farmer's sons. We will tire, we will need to rest, we will get discouraged, but if we keep returning to the task of being present we will reap the reward—a richer, more meaningful life.

"Don't just do something, stand there" is a Buddhist dictum that befuddles the Western mind. This is not a statement encouraging a lackadaisical attitude about life; it is a plea for a posture of presence. Slow down, take your time, be where you are, do what you are doing, feel what you touch, taste what you eat and drink, smell the aromas of life, listen with your heart to what your ears merely hear, and gaze into the depths of what your eyes behold. This is the way of presence, the "technique" that keeps us from missing the Mystery in our midst. Presence is the essential ingredient that makes wonder and contemplation a possibility, for we have to be present if what is here to be sensed is to touch our hearts and move us to live fully.

> "Where shall I look for enlightenment?"
> "Here."
> "When will it happen?"

"It is happening right now."

"Then why don't I experience it?"

"Because you do not look."

"What should I look for?"

"Nothing, just look."

"At what?"

"Anything your eyes alight upon."

"Must I look in a special kind of way?"

"No. The ordinary way will do."

"But don't I always look the ordinary way?"

"No."

"Why ever not?"

"Because to look you must be here. You're mostly some-where else" (DeMello, p. 12).

The enlightenment we look for is not an experience apart from reality but an experience of reality seen in its fullness. The more completely we are where we are, the more likely it is that we will see what is to be seen—that sacredness that abides omnipresent in our midst.

When we are fully present to others, we not only sense their sacredness, we communicate it to them. One of the most significant experiences I have had is that of being heard. The first time I remember being aware of the power of listening was in the context of spiritual direction when I was trying to give voice to the not-so-clear stirrings of the Spirit that I sensed in my soul. Fritz, the person to whom I was speaking, was total-ly present to me. He heard not only my words but my heart as well. I could feel the individual attention with which he entered my confusion. I sensed that, for him, I was the only person in the world at that moment and that that moment and my con-cern was the only thing that mattered. I do not remember what it was that I was dealing with at the time, but I have never forgotten the feeling of being worthwhile that encompassed me in that encounter. We have to be where we are in order to communicate to others and to experience ourselves the profundity of all that we take for granted. It sounds obvious and seems simple, but attempting to live in this manner soon yields the awareness that it takes discipline to be truly present, and that remaining in the present is a less realistic goal than is returning to it when our minds lose their focus.

The act of returning to the present is an art. It involves a nonjudgmental compassion toward ourselves for having wandered from the here and now. It is a gentle reaffirmation of the goodness of living in the moment and being focused on the taken for granted details of our lives. This graceful return is a homecoming, a movement to that place of consciousness where we belong. Becoming aware that we are kidnapped by regrets for past actions, we do not castigate ourselves but simply turn our attention to what is before us. Having gotten trapped by concerns about what is yet to be, we situate ourselves in the perhaps "nothing special nature" of the here and now where Divinity awaits us. It is here in this stack of pots and pans I am washing. It is here in the pages of the book that I must read for tomorrow's class. It is here as I drink my coffee, glance at the newspaper, and drive to work for the one thousandth time. Wherever I am and in whatever I am doing the Holy hides undetected and ever-beckoning.

Patient endurance is a necessary quality of the art of returning to the present because our mind's tendency to wander from it is constant. Hundreds of times a day and every day of our lives we will find ourselves divided—our thoughts in one place and our bodies in another. With time and attention it is possible to be more present more often, but it is the willingness to return our focus to what we are doing and who we are with that is the way of presence.

Being present is as courageous as it is difficult, since much of what we are to be present to in ourselves and in our relationships is not pleasant. It is no picnic to be with another through illness, or to feel the grief that accompanies loss. It is easier to run from the challenges inherent in relationships than it is to work through them. Escaping from loneliness, avoiding the void in the many ways we do so—eating, drinking, sex, television, shopping—is far more appealing than being face to face with it. But the willingness to taste the gamut of life's experiences and not shrink from what is distasteful is to live with integrity, and that treasure can only be found "beneath our own house."

True presence is not just about attentiveness to the world around us, but also to the "world" that is us. We must be present to the physical, mental, and emotional aspects of our selves if we hope to be spiritually enriched. Our bodies require attention; they will distract us from the treasure they hold if we do not feed, exercise, and rest them properly. Our minds can bring us to the edge of mystery only if we discipline them to focus, rather than allowing them to wander. Our emotions can be a rich source of revelation signaling subtle, felt facets of the Essence of us, but they can easily take possession of us, casting us into swings of highs and lows that prevent the stability necessary to stay attuned to our inner depths. Presence requires caring for and about all aspects of ourselves. A dull knife will not cut. A dulled and undisciplined person cannot be fully present to the sacred depth that each moment holds.

In the spiritual life there is no substitute for being present and no easy way to become good at it. We must return to the present as often as we wander from it. This is an art that requires courage and perseverance, both of which are worth our efforts to attain, for the Divine depths whose reality we intuit and long for awaits us here and now.

$\mathcal{T}_{i\,m\,e}$

In our culture we speak about time in many ways: when an outcome is uncertain time will *tell*, when we are having fun it *flies*, when we consider it in relation to financial gain it is *money*, and when it is in short supply, time is *of the essence*.

Time is of the essence, but not just in the sense that there is precious little of it. In relation to the spiritual life, time really is of the Essence, because it is a dimension of the Mystery that lies at the center of all that is, was, and is to come.

The Greek language uses two distinct words to describe two very different notions of time: *chronos and kairos*. Whether it is in reference to the clock (seconds, minutes, hours) or the calendar (days, weeks, months, years) we generally think of time chronologically. This kind of time is measurable, predictable, and inevitable. It is also limited; we have deadlines to meet until we ourselves are dead, that is, until we *run out of time*!

Kairos is another kind of time altogether. It is not a human construct. It has nothing to do with clocks or calendars, but everything to do with the holiness of every moment. Rather than being measurable, it is mysterious. Instead of being predictable, it is full of surprises. It is not so much inevitable as it is inexhaustible. *Kairos* is not concerned with past or future, but only with the abysslike nature of now, with the completeness of the present. This very moment as you sit and read these very words, you are immersed in a vast truth that has neither beginning nor end. This timeless truth does not run out, like chronological time; it runs over. Each instant of each day is bursting at the seams. There cannot be more of now than there is, or more of the timeless Mystery that permeates it. When we consider time as *kairos* it is always the same time, always the occasion for the full recognition of the full presence of the hidden holiness of life.

We experience time as *kairos* when time "stands still," when, for instance, the utter attractiveness of another pierces the armor of a heart once broken. Love at first sight happens at a particular time and on a specific day, but it is a timeless moment. It is a *kairos* moment when we get the tragic news that someone dear to us has died unexpectedly, or when we experience or observe the miracle that is childbirth. These are mesmerizing moments remembered in detail years later, and in them we sense the bottomless, eternal depth that is the font of every moment.

It is difficult to maintain a sense of life's sacredness without an appreciation of time as *kairos*, because the mostly hectic pace of our lives tends to sweep us past the sacred present. There is rarely enough chronological time to accomplish our tasks or attain our goals. In response to this reality, we generally work harder and longer and grow more weary for our efforts. Where, in this lifestyle, is there time to just be, or time to be touched by the Essential nature of time? When we ride on the surface of life, often focused on the past or future, we rarely experience the depth of the present moment. The ability to sense God in the midst of our lives is enhanced by the awareness of time as *kairos*, the unfathomable nature of now.

Living with an awareness of God's presence in the present requires that we resonate with the notion of *kairos* time, but we must also be aware that what we seek is revealed in the context of *chronos*. Seekers are practical people. We live in the world and in time as it is normally understood. We know that we must be aware of *kairos* time if we are to live fully, but that we must be aware of *chronos* time if we are to live responsibly. We run the risk of losing touch with our soul if we only watch the clock, but we know we could lose our jobs if we never consult it. This may appear to be a dilemma, but since *kairos* is at the heart of *chronos*, and because every second ticks in timelessness, we do not need to leave the world of measured time in order to live with sensitivity to life's sacredness. We do not have to throw away our clocks and calendars to appreciate God's presence, but we may have to stop allowing them to rule us, so that we can *spend* time reflecting upon and resting in the eternal now in order to nurture our awareness of it.

In the midst of car pooling, shopping, and housework a young mother sits alone, closes her eyes, and breathes slowly, appreciating the miracle of being alive. While studying in his room, a college student closes his door, turns off the CD player, and reverences the stillness that lies beneath the pressure that so often dominates his awareness. The owner of a small business pauses in the middle of the day, pushes the intercom button on the phone, and strikes a small gong on his desk, the resonant sound of which invites his employees to remember the Mystery incarnate in each moment and every person. These momentary scenarios give witness to the wisdom of *taking* time. They may seem like a waste of chronological time, since their fruits cannot be measured on the scales of productivity, but if this *time out* becomes a part of the rhythm of our day, it need not be at odds with the time required to perform life's many tasks. In any case, seekers know the value of such moments and that we usually emerge from them renewed for the work at hand.

"Eternity" is a word we use to speak about time beyond time, about life that begins when chronological time ends. But in the mind of a seeker, time is eternity disguised as this moment. All time is eternal. Every instant has its beginning in the timelessness we call eternity. I refer again to William Blake for a poetic expression of this truth, in "Auguries of Innocence" (p. 490):

> To see a World in a Grain of Sand
> And Heaven in a Wild Flower
> Hold infinity in the palm of your hand
> And Eternity in an hour.

To live with a sensitivity to the eternity of now is to live in readiness to be surprised by the infinite depth of our finite world. This involves the willingness to be smitten by the sacredness of life as it is, of ourselves as we are, and by the paradoxical endlessness of each passing moment. When we recognize that time is eternity disguised as this moment, and that the present is replete with the Essence of us, we desire to live with vigilance, for what we seek is here; the fullness we usually assign to an afterlife we know to be concurrent with this life.

The opposite of this is an "I can't wait" approach to life. As a child I couldn't wait for school to end and summer vacation begin. I couldn't wait for Christmas and for my birthday so that I would receive the presents that both occasions promised. I couldn't wait to be sixteen so I could get my driver's license, and to be twenty-one in order to drink legally. There was and always is something on the horizon that is difficult to wait for because it appears to offer the satisfaction of our desires. Because time unfolds in the vastness of eternity and eternity is incarnate in the concreteness of time, every moment holds the Mystery that is the fulfillment of our ultimate desire. The challenge for all who seek the Holy in everyday life is to remain awake to its presence now.

When people grow in the awareness of creation's holiness and conform their individual lives to the Spirit that infuses life, they could be thought of as *keeping time* with the Essence of us. Time in this sense is tempo; it is movement in sync with a pulsating presence. Such movement is often slow and rhythmic since it is in keeping with the Divine depths that exist like ocean waters beneath the turbulent surface. But the Spirit can also propel us through life when, for example, we are moved by love's dictates beyond reason's hesitancy. Joseph Campbell states this truth when he says with a touch of humor, "There is a time for Buddhist meditation and a time for Irish whiskey."

No matter what the tempo, it is imperative for spiritual growth that we try to keep time with Mystery's music, "the beat of a different drummer"; however, in so doing we may live in disharmony with our culture. God's tune is a love song that invites us to live not prudently but prodigally, not measuring to whom and how much we give, but opening our hearts to all without holding back.

> "You have heard it said: Eye for eye and tooth for tooth. But I say this to you: offer the wicked man no resistance. On the contrary, if anyone hits you on the right cheek, offer him the other as well; if a man takes you to law and would have your tunic, let him have your cloak as well. And if anyone orders you to go one mile, go two miles with him. Give to anyone who asks, and if anyone wants to borrow, do not turn away" (Mt 5:38-42).

The above is an ancient "song" but it will never be a best-seller. Those who keep time to its beat and live true to its lyrics may be considered foolish at best and subversive at worst. But the beat goes on, and we may find it hard not to tap our feet in rhythm with it because to live in this manner is to be in harmony with our Essence.

Keeping time with the Spirit makes life a great adventure, but it is also a scary ride, since it requires us to relinquish control of our lives. The musical instrument does not set the tempo of a song, the musician does. But even musicians, if they are true to the music they are playing, follow the inspiration of the composer. Faithfulness to God understood as the Ground of Being requires that we read life's music, though we may have a different tune playing in our heads. We must trust that the composer and the composition are one, and that life with all its flats and sharps is both the song and the sound of God.

Primitive religions, it has been said, were not believed, but danced. Spiritual maturity is not a matter of accepting creedal statements, following ritual requirements, or conforming to commanded behavior, though all of these are significant. Rather, it is about reverencing the holy nature of time and living in rhythm with the Spirit's tempo—dancing with the Essence of us.

Simplicity

"Live Simply So Others Can Simply Live" is an adage I have seen on bumper stickers in recent years. It is a good reminder that the proverbial pie of our nation's abundance has a limit, and that the size of our piece of it may mean a lesser portion for others.

Material simplicity has significance for those who seek to touch the Spirit at the core of creation's holiness, since a life cluttered with more than we need can tend to blind us not only to the needs of others, but to the presence of *all that we need*, the one reality which, when we are aware of its indwelling, quiets the desire to clutch those things, people, and experiences we pursue as substitutes for it. The absence of a sense of the Divine within leads many of us on a lifelong, frustrating, and sometimes self-destructive search for meaning, peace, and an ever-elusive happiness. Being true to the pursuit of God in our midst means that we must look within and embrace our longings, rather than looking elsewhere to satisfy them. It would be inconsistent with all that I have written to say that we must reject the material world in order to grow spiritually. Acquisitions or the means to attain them can be distracting, but they are not in themselves barriers to progress on the spiritual path. Many people live simply in the midst of abundance and others who, though they have few things and little monetary wealth, allow what little they do have to consume them. What complicates our lives is not what or how much we have but our attachment to the things we have—being possessed by them rather than being in possession of them.

There was a time in my life when I left the places and people I loved most in order to search for God and myself. I drove a 1978 Honda Civic that was not too much larger than a postage stamp from Indiana to California with all the things I felt were necessary for the journey; there was room to spare in the car. A year later I moved to Chicago with my car filled to the brim. Two years after that I returned to the origin of my journey; not only was my car filled but so was the station wagon of friends who helped me move! By most standards I was living simply, but it struck me then, as it does now, how easily material objects present themselves as essential for "the journey."

Commitment to a life focused on God involves the embrace of simplicity not because the material world is evil, but because we have as a priority the nonmaterial Essence of all that is. Things can be a distraction and thus a complication only if we forget the simple truth of God's indwelling: "For behold, Thou wert within me, and I outside; and I sought Thee outside and . . . fell upon those lovely things Thou hast made. . . . I was kept from Thee by those things . . ." (Augustine, 10, 27). The "lovely things" of this world need not keep us from God, but when they do it is usually because we seek our identity from them, assuming we are worthwhile because of what we have, rather than who we are. Though we continue to fall prey to the lure of things, we eventually sense the futility of finding in them satisfaction for our hearts' longing. When we look within for this satisfaction, our possessions cease to be a problem and can become the joy they are meant to be. When our identity is rooted in our Essence, all that is unessential can be embraced without seducing us by its appeal.

We can more freely let go of what we have when we are aware of the inner richness we possess. There was once a monk who happened upon a priceless gem which he put in his pocket. A thief accosted him shortly after, searched his traveling bag, and found nothing of value. The monk then took the stone from his pocket, gave it to the man, and wished him well. The next day the thief returned, gave the jewel back to the monk, and said, "Take back this jewel and give me what enabled you to let go of it so freely." With regard to material things, seekers live simply by holding lightly all they possess and valuing the Spirit that can never be possessed but can always be given. True simplicity is *freedom from* what we own and the *freedom* to respond generously to what others need; this liberty comes with being in touch with our Essence.

A simplicity detached from the material possessions that are a good and necessary aspect of living in the world can prevent us from being possessed by them. But simplicity is also about detachment from another form of possession having to do with ourselves.

> . . . to be very unobtrusive, and very insignificant, always striving for more simplicity. Yes, to become simple and live simply, not only within yourself, but also in your everyday dealings. Don't make ripples all around you, don't try so

hard to be interesting, keep your distance, be honest, fight
the desire to be thought fascinating by the outside world
(Hillesum, p. 106).

This internal, personal simplicity is about being unencumbered by desires and regrets, by jealousy and grudges. It is freedom from the tyranny of comparisons that flow from the spring
of insecurity and guilt. It is liberation from the need for validation by others. We simply are who we simply are. We have
whatever strengths and weaknesses we have. We are the
product, in part, of whatever experiences have formed us, and
we have been scarred and blessed in the way both have
occurred. All that has occurred has issued in our being the
person we are, and none of it, no matter how beneficial or
damaging, has undone the simple sanctity of our Essence. The
ability to love ourselves as we are enables us to live in the
peaceful, uncomplicated reality of who we truly are.

In order to live with inner simplicity and to see with clarity
the richness that awaits us in our everyday life, we must be
able to abide the imperfect and idiosyncratic person that we
are. The changes that might make us more peaceful within and
better able to live peaceably with others are more likely to
come about not by a process of elimination, but by one of inte-
gration. This is not what I was taught in my youth. I learned
that my faults and failings, large or small, must be purged before
I could rest content with myself. I have engaged in long and
futile interior battles in an attempt to rid myself of what C. S.
Lewis has called "a zoo of lusts, a bedlam of ambitions, a nurs-
ery of fears, a harem of fondled hatreds." I have come to realize
that I can only become who I am meant to be by accepting

who I happen to be, namely, the complex mix of contradictory needs and urges that Merton recognized in himself. He began his autobiography by giving expression to this complexity.

> On the last day of January 1915, under the sign of the Water Bearer, in a year of a great war, and down in the shadow of some French mountains on the borders of Spain, I came into the world. Free by nature, in the image of God, I was nevertheless a prisoner of my own violence and my own selfishness, in the image of the world into which I was born. That world was the picture of Hell, full of men like myself, loving God and yet hating Him; born to love Him, living instead in fear and hopeless self-contradictory hungers (Merton, *The Seven Storey Mountain*, p. 3).

We are light and darkness, virtue and vice, saintly and sinful. We may resent what we dislike about ourselves, but the failure to accept the reality of our complexity can only lead to inner turmoil and outer conflict. The compassionate embrace of who we are issues in a simple at-homeness that allows the light, virtue, and sanctity of ourselves to reign.

Saint Ignatius, the founder of the Society of Jesus (Jesuits), coined a term that I have found meaningful in attempting to achieve inner simplicity: "temptation under the guise of good." Temptation may refer not only to the desire to do something forbidden, but may also apply to what is acceptable, good, and even holy. It is a good and holy thing for us to be rid of envy, pettiness, vanity, a quick temper, and such, but it can also be a temptation not only because success in this venture can lead to spiritual pride but because, as these words of Jesus indicate, "cleaning our house," attempting to perfect ourselves, may be courting trouble:

> "When an unclean spirit goes out of a man it wanders through waterless country looking for a place to rest, and cannot find one. Then it says, 'I will return to the home I came from!' But on arrival finding it unoccupied, swept and tidied, it then goes off and collects seven other spirits more evil than itself, and they go in and set up house there so that the man ends up by being worse than he was before" (Mt 12:43-45).

Being a "simple self," a person at peace within, requires vigilance and resistance to temptation disguised as the impulse to be better than we are. There is always room for improvement, always virtue to attain and vice to be rid of, but it is precisely for this reason that we must learn to accept ourselves as we are, for the grace of change and the grace to change will move within us only if we are not in turmoil, but are, instead, at a restful readiness to grow.

Recognizing the value of self-acceptance for spiritual growth is usually a gradual matter that comes only after we discover that our deepest needs cannot be met without it. We wake up to the truth after being hit over the head with lies! George Bernard Shaw puts it this way: "There are two great disappointments in life; the first is not to get one's heart's desire, the second is to get it." That object, person, or achievement upon which we set our hearts and pin our hopes can never really satisfy us. Likewise, our attempts to improve ourselves rarely bring us the contentment we desire. Because we are spiritual beings, only living in the flow of the Spirit is ultimately fulfilling. This becomes possible when we let go of our self-focus, turn our gaze on the indwelling source of ourselves, and rest in the compassionate mercy that is our Essence.

But the simplicity that comes with acceptance of ourselves as we are does not preclude the fact that some changes may be necessary, that some aspects of our personality and some dimensions of our behavior cannot be tolerated. On the contrary, self-acceptance makes it possible for us to achieve lasting change and steady growth, since these are rooted in self-love. Sessions with a therapist, participation in a weight-loss program, and attending Alcoholics Anonymous meetings are proven means of self-enhancement. But if the motivation for them is disgust with ourselves, our faithfulness to them and their positive effects are likely to be short-lived. When we are possessed by and preoccupied with who we could be and should be, with what we ought to do or cease doing, it is difficult to sustain the disciplines that make us truly healthy. When, however, we enter into those same activities free of negativity and fueled by respect for our sacred selves, we are better able to resist the tendency to hedge on the commitment required to become our best selves.

The simplicity that enables us to hold lightly the things of this world, and to take ourselves lightly as well, is the fruit of having discovered and surrendered to the Essence of us. When we become at home with the truth that all creation is a manifestation of Mystery, we see harmony beneath conflict, commonality beyond differences. Everyone and every thing is a dimension of one reality, and we are in communion with them.

> In the point of rest at the center of our being, we
> encounter a world where all things are at rest in the same
> way. Then a tree becomes a mystery, a cloud a revelation,
> each man a cosmos of whose riches we can only catch
> glimpses. The life of simplicity is simple, but it opens to us
> a book in which we never get beyond the first syllable
> (Hammarskjold, p. 174).

It is from the posture of inner repose that the mystery of
life's depth opens up to us. All things and all people are simply
what they are, but they are profoundly simple, since they bear
in their being the mark of Divinity. "To see God," said George
Washington Carver, "look at anything closely." To see God, the
Ground of Being, look at the ground and all that springs forth
from it: grass, flowers, and trees. Look closely at the sky and all
that moves across it: clouds, birds, and the vapor trail of a passing plane. Gaze into the eyes, the windows of the soul, of the
people we encounter. When we are at the "point of rest at the
center of our being," all these, and all else besides, can be recognized as elements of the one sacred reality they incarnate. To
see this is to see simply. When we see simply we are closer to
living simply.

If, as we seek God, we grow in wisdom, we learn that the
clutter of things can distract us from the awareness of God's
indwelling, that true simplicity is more about being detached than
it is about being without possessions, and that self-acceptance is
key to overcoming the preoccupation that blinds us to the simple
truth that we share a common Essence with all creation.

$\mathcal{S}olitude$

Since it comes with the territory of being human, everyone knows the feeling of loneliness. It is an empty ache; the sometimes acute, sometimes vague sense of not mattering or belonging. It feels like something is missing, though that may not have been the case the day or the hour before. It often comes upon us when we are by ourselves, but can be just as intense in the midst of a crowd. Loneliness is melancholic; it is nostalgic; it is a longing for the home that is solitude.

Robert Frost, when asked to define home, replied, "Home is the place where, when you have to go there, they have to let you in." What Frost is describing is less a physical abode than a web of relationships. Though the actual place we associate with home, our house, is significant, we are most at home when we are with the people who know and care for us. But no matter how strong the bond, how enduring the relationship, or how intense the feeling of connection we may have with others, we cannot escape the periodic sense of loneliness even in the midst of those we love.

As seekers we are only and ultimately at home in the deepest sense when we allow our loneliness to lead us to solitude, that state of oneness with ourselves that is the foundation of the house of our being. Solitude is the inner place of both comfort and conflict, rest and restlessness, where all of who we are is welcome; it is an interior home where we can be alone without feeling lonely. Solitude is communion, it is wholeness, and it is companionship that does not require the presence of another.

It is no mistake or matter of chance that solitude is often experienced in nature. At Genesee Abbey there are acres of woods containing not only countless trees but several lakes and a creek as well. It is a place where I have been lost in a sense of solitude many times. What I have come to realize is that this solitude is reflective of, and perhaps engendered by, the solitude of the place itself. Trees, lakes, and creek are at home in themselves and with one another. They are sacraments of their Essence. In every season of the year, they yield to their nature and flow with the changes that come with the territory of being what they are. Such is human solitude, an at-homeness with ourselves in the seasons of life and in the ups and downs of the day as they give expression to the divine dimension of our being.

When we are at one with ourselves there is room in us for the seasons of joy and sorrow, calm and chaos, clarity and confusion. We may wish that joy, calm, and clarity would take up permanent residence in our soul, but true solitude is a home for every facet of our personality; it consists of who we happen to be at any given point in our life.

When I manage to experience the comfort of solitude, I find it easier to accept the fears, desires, and insecurities that lurk beneath the surface of my consciousness. I am usually able to outrun the awareness of this dimension of myself by seeing to it that there is ample noise and activity to distract me. But when I run out of room to run, when there is nothing left to keep myself from myself, I am confronted with the truth of my imperfection and invited to embrace the whole of who I am. I know at times like this that the Essence of my being is a beneficent, loving, and merciful Mystery that "has to let me in" and does so gladly.

In the same way that we can feel lonely by ourselves or in the company of others, so can we be in solitude in either situation; this is because solitude is an internal reality. It is less a matter of geography—physical separation from the presence of others, and more about biography—being fully present to our true selves. The "place" of solitude is our heart:

> Said the Master to the businessman:
> "As the fish perishes on dry land, so you perish when you get entangled in the world. The fish must return to the water, you must return to solitude."
> The businessman was aghast. "Must I give up my business and go into a monastery?"
> "No, no. Hold on to your business and go into your heart" (DeMello, p. 13).

When we get to the heart of something, we are at its deepest dimension. When we go into our own hearts, we are present to our true self without distraction or illusion. Here we come face to face with who we are and with how our lives are unfolding. Here we discover the truth that beneath whatever inconsistencies may be present, we are one, at the core of our being, with the Mystery we too often and too easily imagine to be separate from ourselves.

Though solitude requires that we enter our hearts, it does not separate us from people. Though it is an encounter with ourselves, it puts us in touch with others. A solitary person is in solidarity with all humanity. It is at the center of ourselves that we are one with all others, since what is the Essence of one is the Essence of all. Oddly enough, we can be more a stranger to others in our daily and often superficial interactions with them than is a hermit whose physical separation is for the sake of intimacy with the inner realm that is our common Ground. This, as Merton points out, is the only valid reason to live apart from others:

> Some men have perhaps become hermits with the thought that sanctity could only be attained by escape from other men. But the only justification for a life of deliberate solitude is the conviction that it will help you to love not only God but also other men. . . .
>
> True solitude is the house of the person, false solitude is the refuge of the individualist. . . . Go to the desert not to escape other men, but in order to find them in God (Merton, *New Seeds of Contemplation*, pp. 52-53).

Solitude and solidarity form a seamless garment; to be truly present to one's self puts us in contact with the other. We cannot relate well to another unless we are able to abide ourselves apart from them. There is no better example of this truth than Merton himself. He describes himself in his early years as someone incapable of true relationship, though he was popular and had many friends. His self-absorption made it impossible to connect on a deep level, in any sustained fashion. It was only after he left the world and, with the help of monastic discipline, entered into the solitude of his soul that he sensed and responded to the common bond he shared will all humanity.

Though the house of our solitude is within us, and is us, it can be difficult to get there.

> In reality, all men are solitary. Only most of them are so averse to being alone, or to feeling alone, that they do everything they can to forget their solitude. . . . By those occupations and recreations, so mercifully provided by society, which enable a man to avoid his own company twenty-four hours a day (Merton, *Disputed Questions*, p. 178).

In order to arrive at and abide in solitude, we have to negotiate streets that lead us in other directions. The city of our society is busy with comings and goings, with work and play, and with hot neon signs that encourage us to live in the fast lane. If our bodies and minds are not occupied, we are considered, by ourselves and others, to be lazy and unproductive. It is difficult in such an environment to rest in the home of solitude without feelings of guilt; how can I just be, when there is so much to do and so many in need? A seeker is drawn to solitude, but responding to this inner imperative is like going the wrong way on a one-way street. We can be labeled a loner, or a recluse, or antisocial when our need to rest in God leads us away from others. Or when, in the company of others, our sense of an inner Presence causes us to "tune out" momentarily, it may appear that we are disinterested in the people or the conversation that surrounds us. "What's wrong with her?" might be an expected reaction. The reality is that there is something right with her; what appears to be distraction is actually preoccupation, an awareness of the occupying Presence that invites her to come home, perhaps fleetingly, while in the midst of daily duties and common conversations. To be at home with her Essence may put her at odds with the ethos of her culture.

But solitude is not just an option for anyone intent on seeking God; it is a necessity. Despite the expectation of an almost constant engagement with others, those who sense the hidden depth of ordinary existence are compelled to be present to it. It is here that we draw strength for our involvements. It is here that we sense meaning in the madness that is life on the run. It is here that we become confirmed in the belief that our own and the world's sanity and sanctity require solitude. Being in this paradoxical place, which Merton calls the "palace of nowhere," an emptiness filled with what alone consoles, allows us to discover what our whole being longs for, namely, an intimacy with God at the center of our self.

Most of us have a tendency to resist the invitation to solitude, the longing to rest in ourselves that arises from our inmost being. Though we know in our hearts its significance, still it is tempting to turn from solitude and to busy ourselves with the work at hand, since the very intimacy we desire is also a threat to our independence. Yet, like the mother I once heard plaintively calling her daughter from play on a quiet spring night, "Kimberly, Kimberly," the summons never ceases—it is always time to come home. Some experience being called to solitude by actually hearing somewhere within themselves the sound of their name spoken as clearly as if another had uttered it. At times the call to solitude comes through the whisper of a deep and subtle sense of discontent with our noisy interactions and nonstop mental conversations. It can be a nameless nostalgia for we know not what that brings us to the brink of solitude, or a sense of compunction for our having wandered so far and for so long from God. And, periodically, we may be called by such a sense of wholeness and gratitude that we must come home to utter a prayer of thanksgiving for blessings undeserved. We are free to turn a deaf ear to the call, however it arises, but to do so is self-defeating. Beneath whatever we are afraid to face, there exists a warmth and oneness in which it is right to rest.

Home, and the sense of belonging and security it stands for, is basic to our emotional health. Solitude, and the communion with our Essence that is its substance, is an interior home we must visit often for the health of our souls and for the sake of solidarity with others.

$\mathcal{R}$ e l a t i o n s h i p

I can think of no arena more vexing or more rewarding than that of relationships. Our interactions with others reveal the worst and the best of ourselves. It is here that we discover the capacity to be both selfish and selfless, the "weeds and wheat" that are a dimension of every person, every seeker.

Priest-psychologist and author Anthony de Mello observes that selfishness is not living our lives in such a way as to make ourselves happy, for that is our responsibility. Rather, selfishness consists in demanding that others live their lives in a way that makes us happy. The impulse to expect others to please us is both strong and subtle. It is second nature to want the people in our life to do and to be as we prefer. We want them to be present to us when we are lonely or in need. We want them to give us space when we feel content or do not want to be bothered by their needs. We want them to want what we want for themselves and for us. We do not usually realize that we are making demands of this sort until it is pointed out to us. This often happens in a confrontational encounter, since such demands can be manipulative and may not be recognized until long-standing patterns have been established.

It is when we are made aware of the selfish nature of our relationships with others that we are invited to examine our relationship with the Essence of us because selfish, dependent, controlling, or abusive relationships are symptomatic of an inner emptiness. They reveal not so much a failure at the art of communication, appreciation, or negotiation—elements of any healthy relationship—but a spiritual malaise, a disease that affects our ability to honor ourselves and reverence others. Our selfishness reveals an alienation from what has been referred to earlier as the "great matter"—the truth of our own and others' holiness—and it leaves us divided within and at odds with those around us. Thomas Moore speaks of this as "loss of soul": "The great malady of the 20th Century implicated in all our troubles and affecting us individually and socially is 'loss of soul.' When soul is neglected it doesn't go away, it appears symptomatically in obsession, addictions, violence and loss of meaning" (Moore, p. xi). The dysfunction that characterizes our interpersonal relationships is symptomatic of an intrapersonal problem, a truth addressed by French philosopher-mathematician Blaise Pascal, who stated that all violence can be attributed to our inability to sit still in a room. If we cannot abide ourselves, how can we live in harmony with others?

> The first and most important intimacy is inner intimacy, the ability to befriend ourselves and embrace our divine depths. ". . . the human encounter depends on an inner connection. To be in touch with you I need to be in touch with me. . . . In intimacy, I am intimate first of all with myself" (Hillman, pp. 37-38).

A healthy relationship with ourselves is what makes for healthy interpersonal relationships, since without self-love we constantly seek signs of approval and validation, a word, a look, a touch, a gift. When these signs are not forthcoming, we either turn on or away from the person(s) from whom we expect to receive them. We become mad or sad; we shout or pout. In any case, we need to affirm our own goodness, and rediscover the soul we may have lost touch with; only then can we stand as a whole person in relation to others.

Being in touch with our soul is key not only to inner peace, but to world peace, as this Chinese proverb indicates:

> When there is peace in the heart there is peace in the
>   home
> When there is peace in the home there is peace in the city
> When there is peace in the city there is peace in the
>   nation
> When there is peace in the nation there is peace in the
>   world.

The lack of peace at all levels has as its source the failure to be in right relationship with the deepest dimension of ourselves, when conflicts arise, the first place to look—though not the only one—is within. Do we expect something from another because we are not at home with ourselves? Are we reacting to their faults because we do not accept our own? Do we project our dark side onto a person, minority group, or foreign nation because we are blind to its presence within? Are we blind to the sacredness of others because we do not see that aspect of ourselves? Hidden in our individual and collective soul lives both our holiness and our hypocrisy, our virtue and our vice. We are at once commendable and contemptible and must embrace ourselves as such; not to do so will inevitably lead to seeing others as a threat, either because their goodness will put us to shame or their shamefulness will make us aware of our own unacceptable self. "Charity begins at home"—to be out of touch and out of sorts with ourselves can only lead to conflict interpersonally and internationally: "War is the spectacular and bloody projection of our everyday life" (Krishnamurti, p. 182).

If selfishness and conflict arise from the failure to be at one with our inherent holiness, then our awareness of this inner sanctuary and our ability to rest in it is what gives birth to self-lessness and harmony. When we truly know who we truly are, we are in a position to let go of self-preoccupation and to live with sensitivity and responsiveness to others. When we are at one with the Mystery in ourselves, we can abide the loneliness, fears, and insecurities that might otherwise lead us to the addictive behaviors and dysfunctional relationships that offer only temporary satisfaction to the permanent longing St. Augustine refers to: "For Thou hast made us for Thyself, and our hearts are restless till they rest in Thee" (I, 1). When we do rest in the embrace of our inner sacredness, we are refreshed and empowered for the work of love that is an expression of the power of God going forth from us to others. But when we attempt to respond to others without "resting in Thee," our own needs for attention, affirmation, and consolation interfere with and complicate our relationships.

Paradoxically, being selfless in relationships requires that we be full of ourselves, that is, filled with the grace of what it means to be ourselves. This fullness is not a prideful consciousness of the way attributes such as intelligence, appearance, or physical strength set us apart from others. Nor is it the awareness that we are generous, sensitive, and intent upon deepening our relationship with God. Rather, to be filled with the grace of what it means to be ourselves is the humble intuition that our preciousness has little to do with ourselves and everything to do with our Essence. It was from the realization of this truth that Mary could utter her Magnificat, "My soul proclaims the greatness of the Lord, and my spirit exalts in God my savior . . . because he has looked upon his lowly handmaid" (Lk 1:46-47). This sort of egolessness allows our God-self to freely function, thus enabling selfless love not only in particular situations, when, for example, we choose to set aside our preferences in order to attend to someone in crisis, but as a constant, for-the-long-haul way of life that is required for responsible parenting, mature marriages, and true friendships.

We are self-centered only when we are not centered in ourselves, that is, not attuned to the Ground of our being, the indwelling presence that is our Essence. When we are one with the oneness of God within, we are free to set aside our own needs and better able to recognize and respond to the needs of others.

Namaste is a term used as a greeting in India; it is a short word with a lengthy meaning:

> I honor the place in you where the whole universe resides.
> I honor the place in you of love, of light, of truth, and of peace.
> I honor the place in you where, if you are in that place in you, and I am in that place in me, there is only one of us.

When we are in the place in us that knows with the heart the vast sacredness we embody, we can be at one with all others, no matter what our differences. Gender, race, religion, sexual orientation, age, socio-economic status, liberal/conservative mind-sets need not be barriers to unity. We are united at the deepest level of our being—that "place in me" where the distinction between me and you dissolves into oneness. Healthy selflessness in relationships is not a matter of disregarding our needs or denying the fact that we are different from and sometimes discordant with others. True selflessness comes with the recognition that I, and others, are more than we appear to be. No longer trapped in my small, ego self, I am free to respond from the depths of who I am to the depths of who they are—person to person, I to Thou, Essence to Essence.

Perhaps the deepest form of relationship we are capable of is that of soul mate. This is what the *Namaste* greeting is about, for to be a soul mate to another requires the willingness to abide the inner sanctum that is the common and holy Ground of all humanity. What a gift it is to meet another at that level. What a blessing to discover in someone a person who knows and values the universal secret of humanity's holiness. How freeing to be able to speak about that great secret without wondering whether we are being judged or misunderstood. The meeting of two or more soul mates is a hallowed meeting. It usually occurs by some combination of fate and chance; we cannot arrange it, but we can prepare ourselves for it by being attuned to our inner depths.

It can be particularly gratifying and exciting to experience a deep, soul connection with a person who, on other levels, may be very unlike us. This makes evident the truth that our spiritual self is our primary self, for it has a vitality and power to bond us to another that is not dependent upon similarity and attraction on a physical, emotional, or intellectual basis. I have been blessed with a number of soul mates over the years. Some of them are women; some are men. Some are older and others younger. Some share my religious tradition; others do not. Rarely are my soul mates just like me. In fact, I have never met some of my soul mates. Some of them died long before I was born; I have become acquainted with them only through their writings. Soul connection is not dependent upon geography or biography, but is a function of "theography," the timeless, spaceless presence of our common incarnate Essence.

The realm of relationships is the place of encounter not only with the best and worst of ourselves, but with the Essence of us as well. We negotiate the spiritual path best when we walk it together. We avoid the pitfall of privacy when we open ourselves to the presence and voice of God that comes through others. Human relationships are an outward manifestation, a sacrament, of the internal communion that is the relationship of humanity and Divinity.

$\mathcal{W}_{o\ r\ k}$

Much is being written these days about spirituality in the workplace, a phenomenon arising from the fact that we spend so much of our lives on the job and often become depleted by it. Whether our work environment is the home or office, factory or store, inside or outdoors, whether the color of our collar is blue or white, many of us come away from our jobs less alive, wishing we had more time and energy for those aspects of our lives that we enjoy.

In his classic book *Working*, street-smart journalist Studs Terkel describes the sober reality that is often life in the workplace:

> This book, being about work is, by its very nature, about violence—to the spirit as well as the body. It is about ulcers as well as accidents, about shouting matches as well as fistfights, about nervous breakdowns as well as kicking the dog around. It is, above all (or beneath all), about daily humiliations. To survive the day is triumph enough for the walking wounded among the great many of us (Terkel, p. xi).

I hope that for most of us these words are an overstatement, and that even if we do not like our jobs, their effect on us is not as negative as his remarks indicate. Work can be creative and dignified as well as violent and deadening, but no matter what its effect, work is what most of us have to do much of the time and most of our lives.

As seekers, our concerns are these: Can the time we spend doing those things necessary to earn the income that enables us to survive and thrive in this brief span of our life enliven us more than it does? Do the efforts we expend to maintain a home and provide for the well-being of those we love have anything to do with the Essence of us? The answer to each is, I think, it depends.

If through our work we are seeking an identity, if we measure our worth by our productivity or bank account, if being busy is the way we feel important or keep from feeling empty, then work may be hazardous to our spiritual health. When we attempt to either find or run from ourselves in a project, we are prone to that dependence, or addiction, that is workaholism. One symptom of this disease is that we become consumed with those responsibilities and personalities that are work-related. Even when we are not on the job, our minds are *working overtime*. Personal relationships suffer, as does our physical, emotional, mental, and spiritual health. We lose the perspective necessary to appreciate the little things, to enjoy life, and to relax in the awareness that our work is a means and not an end.

What I have described and what Terkel addresses is at heart a spiritual problem; it can happen only if we lose touch with who we are, that identity synonymous with the Essence of us. Mobi Ho, a disciple of the Vietnamese Buddhist monk Thich Nhat Hanh, tells about an experience that revealed this truth to her:

> There was a time when I was cooking furiously and could not find a spoon I'd set down amidst a scattered pile of pans and ingredients. As I searched here and there, Thay entered the kitchen and smiled. He said, "What is Mobi looking for?" Of course, I answered "The spoon! I'm looking for the spoon!" Thay answered, again with a smile, "No, Mobi is looking for Mobi" (Hanh, p. x).

This sort of mess and confusion is no stranger to many of us. I recently misplaced my appointment book containing not only the names of the people with whom I had appointments, but also the dates of meetings, weddings, and retreats to which I had committed myself. Frantic is too soft a word to describe the hour it took me to locate my "life." I realized when I took stock of my reaction that my identity had become too tied up with my work and not connected enough with myself. The temporary loss of that book made me aware that I was on the verge of losing my soul.

We fall prey to panic because we have lost touch with our souls. Or is it the other way around? Is the panic and busyness of our lives the cause of our alienation? No matter what the cause, the reality is the same, the state of confusion within and without. No matter what the cause, the cure is the same, discovering within ourselves the truth that intimacy with God gives meaning and purpose to all we do. We can lose ourselves in the frenzy of work, but we cannot find ourselves there, because our identity does not have its source in what we do but in us who do it.

We do not search for ourselves in our work, but we use our strength, intelligence, skills, and concern as an expression of our identity, the source of which is the indwelling Spirit. When we are rooted in and enlivened by the Spirit, we are both animated by our work and radiate life through it; this is evident in the life and work of Travis Ford:

> Laughter rippled from one railroad car to the next, followed by waves of applause. These are sounds not normally associated with the early morning commute. But this was the 7:44 from New Haven to Grand Central Terminal, Travis Ford's train.
>
> Mr. Ford is the convivial conductor who dishes up weather reports, baseball scores, inspirational pep talks and greetings in a dozen languages. . . . Mr. Ford is a folk hero, a font of graciousness in their otherwise rough-and-tumble day.
>
> "He makes everybody smile" . . . "It's refreshing to see somebody who has such a joy for what he does" . . . "You can't help but step off his train with a spring in your step" . . . (Gross, *New York Times*, 1998).

The spiritedness with which Mr. Ford performs his job gives testimony to the Spirit that lies at the core of his being. I have to think that as he enlivens others by the way he "conducts" himself, Mr. Ford is himself nourished spiritually. When we do what we do with love, even on those days we do not love doing it, our work can be a source of satisfaction and our workplace an environment where we, our colleagues, and our customers both give and receive life.

Seeking God in our midst does not mean that we expect to find spirituality in the workplace as if it were a hidden commodity capable of being discovered in the drawer of one's desk. What we seek through work is the opportunity to create an environment where the souls of all who are present will be nurtured. This is not only accomplished by Mr. Ford's brand of enthusiasm; it can also be brought about by a quiet and respectful attentiveness to one's tasks and to the people who share them with us. In a recent National Public Radio broadcast, an employee of a small neighborhood pharmacy that had been sold to a large chain was commenting on how the work atmosphere had changed for the worse after the takeover. "Our old boss," she said, "used to listen to us. He took our ideas seriously." To take others seriously, to refuse to dismiss anyone or to see them as valuable merely for the task they do, to recognize Mystery manifest in ourselves and others, and to enter into every aspect of our work as we would a worship service (the word "liturgy" comes from two Greek words that refer to the work of the citizens of the city-state) is to bring life to the place that may once have drained it from us.

For our work to be spiritually enriching it must be personally satisfying. It is tempting to think that those whose jobs are related to their life's passion, for example, actors, athletes, or artists, can more easily find satisfaction in what they do, but job satisfaction is as much a matter of perspective, meaning, and relationship as it is the use of our talents. We do not have to enjoy the tasks that our jobs entail in order to be enlivened by doing them. What is important is that we are open to the bigger picture wherein we sense that we are a piece of a puzzle and that what we do fits into and contributes to the whole. Without the farmer, no wheat. Without the miller, no flour. Without the baker, no bread. Without the grocer, no access to the bread. This awareness is related to our consciousness of the Ground of Being, for that Ground is the Essence of the wheat, and the flour, and the bread, and all whose hands are involved in its creation, sale, and consumption. We will find our work satisfying and meaningful not primarily because we enjoy it, are good at it, or become wealthy because of it, but because through it we can express and experience the abiding presence of God, a sense of connection and collaboration with others, and the realization that we are making a needed contribution.

In one of his many works, Thomas Merton writes, "You can tell more about a monk by the way he uses a broom than by anything he says." Much can be known about any of us by the manner in which we perform our tasks. Whether at home or away, whether paid for our efforts or not, when we do our jobs wholeheartedly for the good of others, we give expression to what is deepest in us and participate in the ongoing work of creation.

> When we grow radishes in a small container in a city apartment, we participate in creation . . . when we sweep the street . . . we tidy the Garden of Eden . . . when we repair what has broken or paint what is old . . . we stoop down and scoop up the earth and breathe into it new life . . . when we wrap garbage and recycle cans, when we clean a room and put coasters under glasses, when we care for everything we touch and touch it reverently, we become the creators of a new universe . . . (Chittister, pp. 103-4).

When we are fully present to our tasks, our manner of performing them says that God is present to us as we do them. Going through the motions is not the way of one who seeks the Holy in the everyday, for our belief that God is within life enables us to enter the arena of work with energy, determination, and imagination.

My early morning flight out of Colorado Springs was delayed so I decided to have breakfast. As I waited to pay, I noticed the cheerful way in which the cashier was speaking with the customer ahead of me. When he dealt with me in a similar fashion, I said: "Seems like you love your job." He responded, "I love life!" I don't know what, if anything, this man believed about God, but the way he presided over his little corner of creation spoke eloquently about the depth of his spirit and the fact that he had been swept off his feet by life itself. I can't imagine anything more spiritual than that.

Because spirituality is an earthy matter, our spiritual growth is evidenced less by the "odor of sanctity" and more by the odor of sweat; less by the presence of a halo, and more by the calluses on our hands! When we seek God, we do not shrink from hard work, manual or mental, for we know that what we seek is both discovered and expressed by engaging with all our hearts the task at hand.

$\mathcal{P}l\,a\,y$

It is tempting to approach the topic of play merely as the opposite of work, understood in the narrow sense, what we do to make ends meet. Play, then, would be what we do to relax and unwind. It is our outlet, activities undertaken to enjoy ourselves and to recharge our batteries so we can work again!

There is an immense value to play thus understood. It really is regenerative, enabling us to return to our responsibilities with an energy and perspective that is lost when we keep our noses to the grindstone too long. "All work and no play makes Jack a dull boy"—and it doesn't make Jacqueline very interesting either! But play has a deeper meaning; it is an attitude of light-heartedness that is crucial for every seeker, since a too serious and strenuous approach to life serves only to weigh down our spirits. It has been said that angels can fly because they take themselves lightly. If we were to adopt this angelic attitude, we might find ourselves moving more gracefully through life, better able to experience a sacred playfulness in good times and in bad.

When we tap into the Spirit that is our deepest self, we touch the source of our aliveness. This Spirit is, by definition, about movement and lightness. It is dynamic and vital, spontaneous and carefree. To live life with this kind of energy is to be playful even if what we are doing is difficult. An illustration of this truth can be seen in the motion picture *Life Is Beautiful.* The film takes place in the late 1930s and tells the story of an Italian Jew who, along with his wife and young son, is imprisoned in a concentration camp. In an attempt to keep his son from realizing the horror of their circumstances, he chooses to portray a positive attitude, actually making a game out of the various situations that occur. His playful ways did not change the reality of their condition but made it possible for them to ride the surface of its inhumaneness.

Play is a way of living more than it is a type of activity. Much of what we are required to do in our lives—our work, our relationships, our striving for personal and spiritual growth—is sometimes difficult, unpleasant, or in other ways challenging. This makes *how* we do what we do crucial, for if we allow our tasks to dictate our attitude, life becomes a chore and resentment its constant companion. But to choose to enter playfully into what might be difficult can transform both the task and ourselves.

If, to paraphrase the refrain of the song "Come From the Heart," we sing like we don't need the money, we love like we'll never get hurt, and if we dance like no one is watching, perhaps we will discover that life is less taxing and we are more animated. Coming from the heart, living free despite our fears, letting go of the self-consciousness that issues in comparison and self-judgment is no easy matter. It is a decision that may need to be made day by day, event by event, each time we *sing* (use our gifts in the presence of those who may be more gifted), *love* (open ourselves to people who may not appreciate our vulnerability), *dance* (move with the rhythm of our intuitions and relationships, despite the critical observations of family, friends, or society in general). It seems paradoxical, but getting to the point where we can live playfully is hard work that involves self-knowledge and the willingness to risk ridicule.

Merely recognizing the value of a heart-inspired life and a playful spirit does not mean that we can enter into this way of living easily. The ability to be playful seems to be a casualty of the aging process. As necessary as it is for our physical, mental, and emotional well-being to have a little fun now and then, many of us have lost this art that came so easily in childhood. We are serious and logical people, responsible grown-ups. When we do try to play—with others at board games or sports, or alone, jogging or playing video games, for instance— many of us do so competitively and with an intensity that begets tenseness. It is fun only if we win. But it is possible, as singer/songwriter Jimmy Buffet says, to "grow old but not up!" We can stay young-at-heart even as our physical hearts weaken. We can continue to enjoy life at the same time that we take responsibility for ourselves and others. We can have fun whether we win or lose because playfulness is engagement with the Essence of us.

> Do we imagine that when we step into a sailboat, God stays ashore? Or that when we enter a movie, God waits on the sidewalk? Or that when we're in the heat of a tennis match God is waiting in the church pew? We play, it is lovely, and we can revel in God in the midst of our play (Gustin, p. 120).

There is no need to confine God to holy places or religious practices. When we live playfully every place is holy ground and every endeavor is a dance with Divinity. The boundless Spirit we call God goes where we go because it breathes in us. We go where it leads because we are embodiments of it.

We cannot live from our Essence if we are stuck in our ego. We cannot move in sync with the Spirit if we are weighed down with ourselves. Perhaps this is the message of the myth of Adam and Eve, that great story of the Hebrew Scriptures that speaks about the awareness of nakedness as an effect of the original sin that caused Adam and Eve to exit the Garden—playground—of Eden. Work is not the opposite of play; it is, rather, carrying the burden of negative self-consciousness that prevents us from walking lightly and freely through life. This predicament arises for us, as it did for Adam, when we lose touch with the truth that our humanity is holy, that we are always and everywhere in communion with God. Native American spirituality recognizes this truth, as is evident in this saying attributed to the Ojibway Nation: "Sometimes I sit pitying myself and all the while I am being carried by a great wind across the sky." The whole time we sit in self-pity, judgment, or condemnation we are one with the Spirit, the breath of God, the Essence of us, which is, without our knowing it, moving us through the years. When we sit, stand, or walk without this awareness, we do so preoccupied with ourselves, and with a seriousness that makes playfulness impossible.

The awareness of our being carried by the Spirit is often fragile and fleeting. We may experience the truth of the Spirit's support, but still succumb to the tendency to sit in judgment of ourselves, presuming that we should be farther along the path of spiritual maturity. We are often guilty of being too serious, especially about spiritual growth. Many of the people I see for spiritual direction are intent upon becoming more holy, more prayerful, more constantly in touch with God. It is hard to argue with such lofty goals, but unless these goals are held lightly they will never be realized. Buddhists know the wisdom of this approach, which is related in the story about a student who asked the master, "How long will it take me to reach enlightenment?" "Five years," was the reply. "Well, what if I try hard?" the student responded. "Ten years," replied the master!

I know first hand the danger to spiritual growth that seriousness can pose. While doing graduate work in Berkeley, California, in the mid-1970s, I met regularly with a spiritual director. At our first session I launched into an account of my understanding of God and my efforts to pray. Recognizing that I had a case of terminal seriousness, Joe stopped me and said, "What do you do for fun?" I was speechless. I thought for what seemed like five minutes but could make no response—I had forgotten how to have fun. We decided on a game of tennis as a remedy for my dis-ease; I found that while playing I was doing my damndest to beat him! The realization that I had become too serious was the beginning of a radically new and healthy understanding of spirituality. Although I continue to discover myself slipping into seriousness, I now see through the illusion and recognize it for the lie it is. If God is holding the reins, I need to enjoy the ride.

In every other aspect of our lives we have learned that we must put forth effort to attain our goals. To become financially secure, we must work hard and invest wisely. To increase our knowledge, we must study. To build up our physical health, we must exercise. But spiritual growth is another matter. Yes, there is discipline required, steps to be taken to assure that we remain focused, but for the most part we have to learn to stay out of God's way. Spiritual growth is about transformation rather than change. It is not about altering our ways, but being open to the playful, creative ways of the Spirit that bring us to new places in our lives almost without our knowing it. Transformation requires that we relax in our skin and accept the fact that being who we are is enough. It requires the willingness to loosen our grip and to let God lead. Seriousness is a barrier to this process, but a playful spirit enables it.

Because self-consciousness interferes with our ability to be playful, we may well be at our playful/spiritual best when we are engaged in our hobbies, those things we do just for fun or for love. If, for instance, your hobby is wood-working or cooking, you would probably not consider yourself a carpenter or a chef since they are professionals and you are merely an amateur. But theologian Robert Farrar Capon suggests that it is better to be an amateur even at those things we do for a living, since the word amateur means lover. To do what we do for the love of it, and with love for it, is a significant element of playfulness, for then our activity is not only more fun and less self-conscious, but also more nurturing and less draining. Work and fun, life and leisure need not be at odds; when entered into playfully, they are complimentary and may lead to an awareness and experience of the deep truth of God's indwelling.

Ironically, I have experienced the truth of what I write in the writing of it. I envy those who enjoy writing and who seem to do it so effortlessly. Much of the time spent translating my thoughts into the words on these pages has been a chore, hard work and not much fun. However, there have been moments when it just flowed and when I delighted in both the process and the outcome. When I sat to write with a playful spirit, not worrying about how effectively I was organizing and communicating my ideas, time passed quickly and I emerged from my endeavor with energy and a sense of intimacy with God. Strange as it may sound, to see life and to live life like a hobby is the way of one who seeks the deepest truth, for when we are lost in what we are doing, our hearts are more vulnerable to being taken by the Mystery that lies hidden in our day-to-day endeavors.

When we let go, we "let God." When we sing, love, and dance without the burden of self-consciousness, we are most alive. When we do what we do for the love of it, we move beyond our ego selves and into the playful experience of life and of a deeper self, one that is one with the Essence of us.

$\mathcal{D}eath$

"Is there life after birth?" is a question once posed in a sermon by a priest-friend. Most people presumed it was a Freudian slip and that he meant "life after death," but the question was meant as stated, and the point was to get the congregation to reflect on the quality of their lives. Were they merely existing, were they "dead men (and women) walking," or were they truly alive: vital, passionate, compassionate? It has been said that pain is inevitable, but suffering is an option. Existence is a given, but being fully alive is a decision.

My experience with those for whom spiritual growth is a priority is that the death that concerns them most is the one that happens this side of the grave. I once thought that by the time I was in my mid-fifties I would sense the nearness of death and reflect a good bit on its inevitability. Having reached that point in good health, I find that I give very little thought to my physical death, but a good deal to its spiritual counterpart. The former, though it may intrude at any time, seems far less real than does the living death, that is, life apart from the Essence of us.

How do we die this death? How do we keep from succumbing to it? "We die on the day when our lives cease to be illuminated by the steady radiance, renewal daily, of a wonder the source of which is beyond reason" (Hammarskjold, p. 56).

When we follow the beaten path instead of responding to the beat of a "different drummer," when we live in our heads rather than with our hearts, when we bow to convention—societal, familial, or religious—without standing in the light of an inner radiance, we are spiritually dead, neither aligned with nor enlivened by the source of our sacredness. This living death may be well disguised even from ourselves, because our lives will probably look like those of most others. We will likely have more good days than bad. We will have our share of successes. We will experience some happiness, some semblance of peace, and the comfort of knowing that we are normal.

But are we normal? Is anyone just normal? Or are we not unique in our normalcy, different in our alikeness? Are we not called to experience the fullness of our lives, the vibrancy that can only come with opening to the "steady radiance" that is the Essence of all of us? Living this way may not lead any of us to the uniqueness that is the status of celebrity, but that is not the point. What matters is that within the apparent normalcy of our lives, we are enlivened by the Spirit, animated by the living God alive in us and moving us with a gradual inevitability to be the persons we are both called to become and capable of becoming. No matter what our age or circumstance, the option is always before us: we can decide to merely exist or to live.

About a year before her death, I met a woman who exhibited in a most difficult situation that there can truly be life after birth. Rita, a cancer patient, was unhappily married. She was at odds with one of her daughters, and upset about the abusive relationship that another of her children was in. She was concerned that when she died her family would disintegrate. She lived in constant pain both during and outside of her admissions to the hospital. But despite the weightiness of her physical condition, emotional concerns, and imminent death, Rita was very vital. She meditated daily, busied herself with baking and knitting gifts for the people she loved, and buoyed up those who were upset with the reality of her Job-like existence. Her connection with her soul enabled Rita to resist the gravitational pull of her circumstance. She refused to die spiritually before she died physically.

The clinical name for spiritual death is depression. There are many causes and kinds of psychological depression, but the feeling of emptiness, the loss of meaning, the inability to concentrate, and the lack of energy that characterize most forms of clinical and situational depression are also symptoms of the gradual death that results from being out of touch with our Essence. Whether we call it depression or spiritual death, the reality is the same; we exist rather than live.

Along with medication and therapy, one of the means prescribed to counter the effects of depression is physical exercise, which causes the release of endorphins, a chemical of the brain that induces a feeling of well-being. The living death that results from being out of touch with the Spirit is countered by interior as well as physical exercise. In order to maintain and to strengthen our awareness and experience of the communion with God that is the font of our lives, we must spend time and expend energy promoting our spiritual health. We do not, by our efforts, create the union with God that is the difference between merely existing and being fully alive, but how we live and think does affect that bond and our awareness of it. We will consider some spiritual "exercises" in the final chapter of this book, but for now we will focus on attitude, since how we posture ourselves mentally is crucial for the well-being of our soul. Inclusivity, compassion, and gratitude are three attitudes that enable us to combat spiritual death.

It can be comfortable and secure to close our minds and hearts to people or ideas that are different, challenging, or threatening, but a refusal to open ourselves to the new and unknown results in a spiritual malaise. The Spirit at the center of our being is by nature vibrant and boundless; it urges us toward openness. To live in communion with it we must resist the temptation to settle in, or to settle for any form of individualism, racism, parochialism, nationalism, and the like. To succumb to these is to exist entombed in narrowness, limited to a life cut off from the richness of diversity. We are one family enlivened by the same spirit. Our differences are real but it is our attitudes about them that makes them either a barrier or a blessing.

When we exclude others, we limit ourselves. But we live at one with our common Essence when the circumference of our life embraces all.

> He drew a circle that shut me out
> Heretic, rebel, a thing to flout
> But love and I had the wit to win
> We drew a circle that took him in.
> —Markham, "Outwitted" (p. 67)

It is tempting to draw circles that close out those who do not share our values, affirm our choices, or those we simply do not like. We naturally spend most of our time with people whose company we enjoy, but when we allow this tendency to close us off from the challenges that come with diversity, we limit ourselves and become less alive.

The life-enhancing virtue of *inclusivity* involves not only our relationship to others, but to ourselves as well. When we refuse to embrace ourselves as the imperfect persons we are, we exercise a form of exclusivity that drains us of life. If we are only acceptable to ourselves without our anger and greed, pettiness and pride, we are a house divided and will surely fall. To be spiritually alive we must learn to befriend even those aspects of ourselves that appear to be "a thing to flout," thus enabling ourselves to learn from them rather than to be ruled by them. If, for instance, I attempt to root out my inclination toward angry outbursts, I fail to recognize that the problem is not my temper or my impatience with the faults of others, but my inability to tolerate my own shortcomings. My anger teaches me that I must be more compassionate toward myself. When I adopt this attitude I find that I am less angry, less drained, and more alive.

If we do not ingest food we will die. If we do not stimulate our minds, we become dull. If we exclude people from the circle of our relationships and aspects of ourselves from ourselves, we will never be the fully alive persons we are capable of becoming.

Equally important for the life of our soul, and just as consistent with the Spirit's nature as inclusivity, is the attitude of *compassion*. Formed by the two Latin words, *cum pati*, compassion means "to suffer with." It is more than sympathy for another in their plight, for compassion implies oneness. Our differences are real, but not as real as the Essence we share in common. When we live with a sense of compassion, people matter to us; we resonate with what happens to others, and we respond to them, for although we are separate from one another at the level of our bodies, we are one at the level of our being. Perhaps, like me, you may wonder whether you are a compassionate person when you pass, without giving, a homeless person asking for spare change. The fact is that something in us usually does respond to them, and we are all too aware that but for circumstances our roles could be reversed. I know that even when I do give the hoped-for handout, I am not someone helping another who is disadvantaged, but one who is poor and homeless in a less obvious and immediate way. Compassion may not always lead us to give what is needed, but it always knows there is a connection between us and the other.

Compassion serves to slow us down. Many of us speed through our days going from task to task, encounter to encounter, never realizing the depth of connection that bonds us with the world and with others. I find that children are great teachers when it comes to compassion. Taking a walk with a young child is not a matter of getting from one place to another, but of discovering along the way the Mystery manifest in a leaf lying on the ground or a dog met along the way. It is as if the child recognized that these things are companions on life's journey. They cannot be passed by but must be met, examined, and related to, since they all—leaf, dog, child, and the adult whose hand the child holds—share a common Essence.

Spiritual death derives, in part, from a sense of emotional separateness. Compassion bridges the gap and gives life to us and to those who are its catalysts. Others may never know of our sense of communion with them, but whether known by them or not, compassion breathes life into our souls and keeps the living death of indifference at bay.

Gratitude also promotes the life of our soul. In its most profound meaning, gratitude is much more than being thankful for what pleases us. True gratitude is the willingness to embrace whatever occurs in our life, pleasing or not. It is radical, flying in the face of conventional wisdom. It says life is good even when it hurts, and that even our physical death is a dimension of a deeper life. A grateful life is a gracious life, because gratitude enables us to move with ease, not resisting but accepting the whole of our lives.

David Steindl-Rast, a Benedictine brother and spiritual writer, speaks about the relationship between gratitude and happiness. He says that happiness generally gives rise to gratitude. When things go as we wish, we are grateful for that fact. Since life has a way of resisting our best efforts to control it, we are usually happy and therefore grateful only some of the time. Steindl-Rast indicates that spiritual health is evidenced when gratitude elicits happiness. When we willingly embrace the reality of our lives as they are, our happiness does not depend on what happens, but is a byproduct of the willingness to receive and to deal with what is.

Gratitude looks like parents accepting with awe and with love the infant born with a defective heart. It looks like that same child years later who, having survived its infirmity, now tends with reverence to the aging parents afflicted with Alzheimer's. Gratitude looks like us when, without knowing why life has unfolded as it has, we embrace the blessing and the curse of it all, realizing that by doing so, we are happier than we could have ever imagined.

Gratitude rests on the belief that whatever is happening should be happening. This is not to say that when violence reigns it is right or should merely be tolerated. What it does affirm is that reality is what it is, and we are called not to bemoan but to address it. A person alive with gratitude grabs the bull of interpersonal conflict by the horns and initiates conversation with the people with whom he clashes. A grateful person does not waste time procrastinating in the face of an undesirable task but takes hold of it instead, aware that in doing so she is opting for life. Gratitude recognizes the need to be engaged in life and to discover the Essence of us that lies hidden in the midst of good times and bad.

I now turn briefly to the death that is the cessation of our bodily being. I say briefly because, despite the accounts of those who have "come back" from it, there is not much anyone knows about what awaits us when we die.

Like others, seekers experience the natural fear that accompanies the thought of death. This can be fear of the unknown, fear of physical pain, or the fear associated with the belief that we will be judged harshly for a life lived imperfectly. But if death is felt to be an unencumbered participation in the life of the Spirit, these fears are not daunting. Even a life lived to the full here and now, one lived in good health, with compatible relationships, and in material comfort, is a life lived within the limits of time, space, and bodies. When we sense that life is larger than life as we know it, the fears associated with death lose some of their power. When we recognize that our physical death is not so much a ceasing to be as it is a being without ceasing, we can tolerate and even embrace the dying process, both the daily demise that is apparent when we gaze into the mirror at our "not what they used to be" bodies, and the final days that are the last stage of terminal illness.

I believe death to be the infinite experience of the disappearance of life's limits, a free-fall into the endless bliss of Being, a coming home to the spacious rapture that we now glimpse dimly and experience peripherally when we live from the heart and in the embrace of the Essence of us.

We die spiritually when we lose touch with the "steady radiance . . . of a wonder" within us. But there can be life after birth if we live with an open and inclusive mind, a compassionate heart, and an attitude of gratitude.

$\mathcal{S}_{p\,i\,r\,i\,t\,u\,a\,l}$ $\mathcal{P}_{r\,a\,c\,t\,i\,c\,e}$

In the preceding pages I have called seekers those who are drawn to the sacred depth of reality. This attraction is dramatic in some people and subtle in most. Though we are free to resist its gravitational pull, its persistence is formidable. To surrender to it implies a willingness to order our lives around the central truth that because God is the Essence of us, humanity and indeed all creation is holy.

In order to be attuned to this "great matter," seekers adopt a spiritual practice that consists of one or more activities that serve to engender an awareness of God's incarnate presence. In this chapter I will present various endeavors, some combination of which could comprise a person's spiritual practice.

Prayer/Meditation We have already reflected on prayer, which is by far the most significant element of a spiritual practice. This is because listening, which is so central to prayer, is a key ingredient in all the endeavors that make up one's practice. We must enter into the various forms of our practice prayerfully if they are to deliver us to an awareness and experience of life's sacredness.

The term "meditation" is used in a variety of ways. It sometimes refers to mental prayer, the process of reflecting on a passage of scripture, some aspect of the life of Jesus, the Buddha, etc., or of one's own life in relation to spiritual growth. Meditation can also refer to that form of virtually wordless prayer that involves, for instance, the silent recitation of a mantra (a repetitive word or phrase), or the awareness of one's breathing while sitting in silence and stillness. When meditating in this manner, it is considered best not to think about our thoughts or feelings but merely to acknowledge their presence and gently return to our mantra or breath as a vehicle for being fully present to the sacred Presence in which we sit. It is generally thought that two twenty minute periods of intentional prayer/meditation a day is an effective means of promoting a prayerful life. I refer the reader to *The Contemplative Heart* by James Finley for an in-depth consideration of meditation.

Religious Devotions Whether done in private or with others, traditional religious devotions are for many a way to sustain themselves on their spiritual journey. Regular participation in church or temple services, pilgrimages to holy places, celebrating the various liturgical seasons (Advent, Christmas, Lent, Easter, Pentecost) of the Christian calendar, or the Jewish High Holy Days, honoring saints, reciting prescribed prayers, and praying the rosary are all examples of devotional practices. Every faith tradition has its treasure of these.

Spiritual Reading Sometimes referred to by its classical name, *lectio divina*, prayerful reading of scripture is an age-old practice. This meditative process involves quietly reading a passage until you are struck by a word or phrase. At that point you stop reading and allow the meaning or feeling that accompanied the words to penetrate your heart. You reverently ponder your thoughts and experience your feelings, formulate a prayer that gives expression to them and finally just sit still in the truth that, through what you have read you are being invited into communion with life's sacred source the fullness of which no words can express. Although *lectio* is generally done with scripture, many may on occasion find other spiritual writing more nourishing. It is not unreasonable to think that the newspaper or the events of one's life can provide the subject matter for a *lectio*. The important thing is not what is read, but the openness and vulnerability with which we approach a book, person, or our lives. *Lectio* can be done alone or in a group setting; the latter allows the opportunity to discuss with others the experience of one's prayer.

Journaling Those inclined toward writing may find keeping a journal a powerful way to stay in touch with the Spirit. Writing about the day's activities and one's reaction to them can uncover the otherwise hidden Presence at the sacred center of life. One form of journaling, "active imagination," involves an inner dialogue. Sitting with pen and paper you ask God, a person in a dream, or another significant figure a question. Without thinking about it, you write that person's response as it comes to you. Continue by writing another question or comment in response to what you just wrote. Allow this dialogue to go on as long as it seems fruitful. It is often amazing what wisdom this process unearths in us. Ira Progoff's *At a Journal Workshop* describes a method of journal writing that has proven beneficial for many who seek God within.

Dreams Many seekers know the value of dreams as a way of discerning the Spirit's movement. Dreams present us with the symbol-rich content of our unconscious. They can reveal to us the inner workings of our soul and give us important information about our deepest needs and fears. Some find it best to get up during the night to write the details of a dream or dream fragment. Some wait until the next morning, hoping they will remember most of the dream's content. Still others, using a tape recorder, literally record their dreams in a half-conscious state during the night. It is not necessary to thoroughly analyze our dreams in order to benefit from them. Sometimes it is enough just to be in touch with the feelings they evoke. *Inner Work: Using Dreams and Active Imagination for Personal Growth* by Robert Johnson is a good resource for anyone wishing to become proficient at learning from their dreams.

Labyrinth A labyrinth is a circuitous path leading to a central point. It is symbolic of life's journey with its twists and turns, and the spiritual, inward pilgrimage that brings us face-to-face with our sacred center. Walking the labyrinth is an ancient meditative practice; its effects are both spiritually quieting and physically relaxing. Though labyrinths, both indoor and outdoor, are generally walked, some people find it more convenient to use a hand-held labyrinth whose path is followed by tracing the design with one's finger. *Walking a Sacred Path: Rediscovering the Labyrinth as a Spiritual Tool* by Lauren Artress provides a good overview of this spiritual practice.

Fasting In years past, fasting was thought of as mortification or self-punishment. "More pain, more gain" was the thinking about spiritual growth that led to this understanding of fasting. Some find that periodically refraining from food not only cleanses their bodies, but also serves as a reminder of a deeper, spiritual hunger. Fasting is sometimes practiced in conjunction with times spent in solitude or retreat. Though usually thought of in relation to food, we may fast from any thing, activity, or person whose place in our lives keeps us from the awareness of our Essence.

Retreats Many aspects of a spiritual practice are entered into on a frequent, sometimes daily basis. Periodically it can be helpful to pull away from the familiar patterns and context of our lives in order to focus more intently on their holiness; a retreat experience can *kick start* our spiritual life. There are a number of different types of retreats. A preached retreat is a group experience where participants attend talks on specific spiritual topics. A private retreat gives one time and space to be alone for prayer, reflection, and, perhaps, needed naps! A directed retreat is similar to a private retreat except that the retreatant meets daily with a director who, along with providing a listening ear, may suggest books, scripture passages, or other forms of input to enhance the retreat experience. A sesshin is a Buddhist retreat comprised mainly of long hours of meditation and, usually, the opportunity to meet briefly with a "teacher." A contemplative retreat is characterized by silence. There are sometimes brief conferences on the spiritual life, and, if experienced in a monastic setting, the opportunity to participate in the rhythm of common prayer (perhaps five or six times a day) with the monks.

Besides the general types of retreats just described, there are also retreats for specific groups: alcoholics, married couples, singles, those with terminal illness, and so on. These can be of value because our spiritual life is intertwined with the rest of our life; it affects and is effected by the whole of who we are. Retreats of this nature can introduce us to others who share our life circumstance and may be a source of affirmation and support.

It may be impractical, if not impossible, to take a week, a weekend, or even a day for a retreat. In this case, or along with periodic retreats, attending lectures or discussions on topics pertaining to spirituality can be a more accessible way to enhance our growth. Prior to these experiences, it is helpful to remind ourselves that it is not just information, but transformation we seek.

Spiritual Direction Monthly meetings with a spiritual director, someone sensitive to the ways of God and skilled in the ways of people, is a valuable asset to anyone who wants to plumb the depths of their soul. A director—also called a spiritual friend, guide, or companion—provides the opportunity to discuss all phases of one's life. Together the directee, and the director (who is also a seeker) attempt to discern how the relationships and circumstances in the directee's life are related to their spiritual growth. Unlike therapy, the focus of these sessions is not problem-centered, but Spirit-centered. They are not about us, our ego selves, but about our relationship to the Mystery that moves within and among us.

Service Because the Essence of one person is the Essence of all, attending to others can open our eyes to the incarnate nature of God. Without overlooking the spiritual dimension of caring for those we love, caring for those most in need has special significance. To recognize the Holy in people we are drawn to may come easily; to see that same reality in those whose person or circumstances are less attractive requires maturity. Regular involvement on behalf of those on the margins of society may help us to see them as persons, spiritual beings not just statistics, and prompt us to regard ourselves as like them, except for the differences in our particular and perhaps temporary circumstances.

These spiritual practices are all tried and true means to spiritual growth. Faithfulness to one, some, or all of them requires discipline. But there are other activities equally beneficial, though they may demand less effort; this is so because they are activities which, due to our temperament, interests, and skills, we might find enjoyable. These too can be elements of a spiritual practice because, like those already mentioned, they can be the source of our awakening to the Holy, and nourishment for our souls.

Nature "The world is charged with the grandeur of God" (Hopkins, "God's Grandeur," p. 70). The grandeur of creation can provide an overpowering experience of the grandeur of God. Many people are drawn to nature—oceans, mountains, deserts, forests—because these places can ignite a sense of awe and a feeling of union with creation. Gazing at the stars or the moon, watching the sun rise or set can banish any doubt that there is a Divine dimension to all reality. For those who are vulnerable to nature's ability to reveal this truth, being in natural surroundings can be a beneficial spiritual practice.

Relationships Spending time with those we love, whether that time is pure enjoyment or the effort necessary to deepen our bond with them, is holy ground. When the parties in the relationship discover a mutuality in their interest in spiritual growth, their togetherness can occasion a deepening in their awareness of and appreciation for God incarnate in each of them. When a relationship is a catalyst for the growth of our souls, then availability and vulnerability to another can be considered a dimension of our spiritual practice. Spiritual friendship honors the mystery of each person, offering both acceptance and challenge as each party freely discloses the contents of their hearts and, in the process, the presence of Divinity. What Rainer Maria Rilke says about love is an apt description of spiritual friendship: "Love is this: that two solitudes border, protect, and salute one another" (p. 59).

Recreation We have already considered the significance of those activities we do just because we enjoy them. These too can be considered a spiritual practice because by involvement in them we can be delivered to the Essence of us. Music, either performed or listened to, can do this. So can gardening, knitting, painting, drawing, swimming, jogging, yoga. What delights and relaxes us can be a means of awakening to the deep current of the Spirit's flow within. Recreation can re-create in us an awareness or experience of intimacy with God.

Pertinent to the consideration of our spiritual practices is the importance of taking care of ourselves. The Spirit is a boundless reality, but it is also an embodied one. Just as we can bring our spiritual resources to bear in the quest for physical and emotional health and healing, so those dimensions of us, if sound, can enhance our spiritual well-being. In order to glean the most from our spiritual practices, it is important to care for our bodies. Proper diet, rest, and exercise enable us to be more alert and more fully present to our spiritual practices. It is important to address our emotional needs and to befriend our feelings—be they welcome or not—because they will be less likely to distract us if they are acknowledged and embraced. This carries over into the realm of relationships, for when we fail to deal honestly and promptly with our feelings toward others, we become preoccupied with the feelings and thus less available to the sacred present.

The array of activities we choose will probably change at different times as our needs change and as we grow. It is important not to undertake them merely as tasks that will help us become more spiritual. The point of a particular practice is to become more aware that we are already spiritual beings, and to enable us to enter into our day and our life responsibly, reverently, and passionately.

$\mathscr{P}ostscript$

Every person has an innate longing for that which is ultimate and infinite. Seekers are moved in a conscious and intentional manner to hold this desire as a priority and to pursue its fulfillment.

Traditionally, we have been taught to look beyond this life and our world for the satisfaction of this inner urging. Although our final and fullest communion with the Holy may lie beyond life as we know it, seekers are not content to look toward a future time or distant place to satisfy a present imperative; we cannot hold our breath until our death and still respond to the call to be alive here and now.

To know the Mystery in our midst, we must focus on the present, for what lies beyond also dwells within. And so we attempt to live with a penetrating awareness of the present, believing our *holy hunch* is true; namely, that every person, every thing, every sight and sound is somehow a sacrament of the Sacred, a revelation of the Mystery referred to by the word "God." We know that what we seek is already a reality and that we live "steeped in its burning layers." Though we are aware that we cannot see the full brightness or feel the complete extent of Divinity's warmth in our lifetime, we continue to strive for a glimpse of God, and rejoice in the sometimes felt sense of a Presence that assures us our search is not in vain.

In the last analysis, however, it is not we who seek but we who are sought. C. S. Lewis noted, "people seeking God is like a mouse seeking a cat!" The fact that we have an inkling that there is a hidden and holy depth to creation is an indication that that very depth abides in us and moves us toward a recognition of, and a surrender to, its permeating presence. In coming to this realization, seekers tend to slow down, to lighten up, to trust that life is leading us where we need to go, for we are not only sought, we have been caught!

May we be faithful to the search, the blessed undertaking that is the God-inspired pursuit of God, and may we be willing to be "taken under" by the pursuing God whose Being is the Essence of us.

$\mathcal{B}ibliography$

Artress, Lauren. *Walking a Sacred Path: Rediscovering the Labyrinth as a Spiritual Tool*. New York: Riverhead Books, 1995.

Augustine of Hippo. *The Confessions of Saint Augustine*. Translated by F. J. Sheed. New York: Sheed & Ward, 1942.

Beck, Charlotte Joko. *Nothing Special: Living Zen*. San Francisco: Harper, 1993.

Blake, William. *The Complete Poetry & Prose of William Blake*. Edited by David V. Erdman (2nd edition). New York: Anchor Books, 1982.

Bolen, Jean. *Tao of Psychology*. San Francisco: Harper, 1982.

Borg, Marcus. *The God We Never Knew*. San Francisco: Harper, 1997.

_____. *Jesus in Contemporary Scholarship*. Valley Forge: Trinity Press International, 1994.

Buechner, Fredrick. *A Room Called Remember*. San Francisco: Harper Collins Publishers, Inc., 1984.

Chittister, Joan. *There Is a Season*. Maryknoll, New York: Orbis Books, 1995.

DeMello, Anthony. *One Minute Wisdom*. New York: Doubleday, 1988.

_____. *Song of the Bird*. New York: Doubleday, 1984

Dillard, Annie. *Pilgrim at Tinker Creek*. New York: Harper Collins Publishers, Inc., 1974.

Finley, James. *The Awakening Call*. Notre Dame, Indiana: Ave Maria Press, 1984.

———. *The Contemplative Heart*. Notre Dame, Indiana: Sorin Books, 2000.

Gross, Jane. "Before Daily Grind, A Human Touch." *New York Times*, 18 October 1998, sec. 1, p. 31.

Gustin, Marilyn. *We Can Know God*. Liguori, Missouri: Liguori Publications, 1993.

Hammarskjold, Dag. *Markings*. With a foreword by W. H. Auden. New York: Alfred A. Knopf, 1964.

Hanh, Thich Nhat. *The Miracle of Mindfulness*. Boston: Beacon Press, 1975.

Hillesum, Etty. *An Interrupted Life*. New York: Washington Square Press, 1981.

Hillman, James. *In Search: Psychology and Religion*. New York: Charles Scribner's Sons, 1967.

Hopkins, Gerard Manley. *Poems of Gerard Manley Hopkins*. Edited by W. H. Gardner (3rd edition). New York: Oxford Press, 1948.

Keen, Sam. *Apology for Wonder*. New York: Harper & Row, 1969.

Johnson, Robert. *Inner Work: Using Dreams and the Active Imagination for Personal Growth*. San Francisco: Harper & Row, 1986.

Krishnamurti. *The First and Last Freedom*. Wheaton, Illinois: Theosophical Publishing Company, 1968.

Markham, Edwin. *The Best Loved Poems of the American People*. Edited by Hazel Fellman. New York: Doubleday, 1936.

May, Gerald. *The Awakened Heart*. San Francisco: Harper, 1991.

Merton, Thomas. *The Asian Journal of Thomas Merton*. Patrick Hart and Naomi B. Stone, eds. New York: W. W. Norton and Company, Inc., 1988.

_____. *Day of a Stranger*. Salt Lake City, Utah: Gibbs M. Smith, Inc., 1981.

_____. *Disputed Questions*. New York: Farrar, Straus & Cudahy, 1960.

_____. *New Seeds of Contemplation*. Norfolk, Virginia: New Directions Publishing Corp., 1962.

_____. *The Journals of Thomas Merton, A Search for Solitude, Vol. III*. Lawrence Cunningham ed. San Francisco: Harper Collins Publishers, Inc., 1996.

_____. *The Seven Storey Mountain*. New York: Harcourt Brace and Company, Inc., 1948.

Moore, Thomas. *Care of the Soul*. New York: Harper Collins Publishers, Inc., 1992.

Progoff, Ira. *At a Journal Workshop: Writing to Access the Power of the Unconscious and Evoke Creative Ability*. Los Angeles: Jeremy Tarcher, 1992.

Rilke, Rainer Maria. *Letters to a Young Poet*. Translated by M. D. Herter Norton. New York: W. W. Norton & Company, Inc., 1954.

Shannon, William. *"Something of a Rebel": Thomas Merton, His Life and Works*. Cincinnati: St. Anthony Messenger Press, 1997.

Terkel, Studs. *Working: People Talk About What They Do All Day and How They Feel About It*. New York: Pantheon Books, 1974.

Wordsworth, William. *Selected Poetry of William Wordsworth*. Edited by Mark Van Doren. Modern Library Edition. New York: Random House, 1950.

Tom Stella is the cofounder of the Soul Link
Center in Colorado Springs. The purpose of the
center is to create opportunities for spiritual
seekers to meet one another and enhance their
journey through retreats, study, spiritual direction,
small group discussions, and community service.
Stella, a priest in the Congregation of Holy Cross,
also leads a spirituality in the workplace program
and serves as a hospital chaplain. He holds a
master's degree in counseling from the University
of Michigan, a Master of Divinity from the
University of Notre Dame, and a Masters in
Theology from Graduate Theological Union in
Berkeley.